Juanita Phillips

A PRESSURE COOKER
SAVED MY LIFE

Juanita Phillips

A PRESSURE COOKER
SAVED MY LIFE

*how to have it all, do it all
and keep it all together*

DESIGN MARIO MILOSTIC
www.mariomilostic.com

ABC
Books

ABC Books

The ABC 'Wave' device is a trademark of the Australian Broadcasting Corporation and is used under licence by HarperCollins*Publishers* Australia.

First published in Australia in 2010
by HarperCollins*Publishers* Australia Pty Limited
ABN 36 009 913 517
harpercollins.com.au

HarperCollins*Publishers*
25 Ryde Road, Pymble, Sydney, NSW 2073, Australia
31 View Road, Glenfield, Auckland 0627, New Zealand
A 53, Sector 57, Noida, UP, India
77–85 Fulham Palace Road, London W6 8JB, United Kingdom
2 Bloor Street East, 20th floor, Toronto, Ontario M4W 1A8, Canada
10 East 53rd Street, New York NY 10022, USA

National Library of Australia Cataloguing-in-Publication entry
Author: Phillips, Juanita.
Title: A pressure cooker saved my life / Juanita Phillips.
ISBN: 9780733325885 (pbk.)
Subjects: Pressure cookery.
Quick and easy cookery.
Dewey Number: 641.587

Cover and internal design by Mario Milostic
Typeset in 11.25/16.5pt Adobe Caslon Pro by Mario Milostic
Manufactured in China by Phoenix
Printed on 140gsm Woodfree

6 5 4 3 2   10 11 12 13

In loving memory of Karmelo Milostic

By the time a man realizes
        that maybe his father was right,
  he usually has a son
      who thinks he's wrong.

Charles Wadsworth

acknowledgements

THIS BOOK OWES ITS EXISTENCE to two remarkable women. My literary agent, Selwa Anthony, gave me the gentle (but firm) encouragement I needed to keep writing at a time of family crisis, and continues to inspire me with her positive outlook on life. My mother-in-law Marija Milostic has been our main pillar of support since our children were born, and generously devoted countless hours to cooking meals and minding children so we could complete this project.

I am also grateful to the many people who have shared their personal stories of the work/life juggle with me, including the complete strangers who have poured their hearts out at parks and playgroups; to John Phillips and Euleen Stanford for their help with historical research; and Gaye Phillips for her help in conquering the Mixmaster and the pressure cooker. My sister-in-law, photographer Helen Coetzee, contributed many hours and some beautiful images; and Simon Blazey cheerfully gave up several weekends to help with production. Thanks also to Annette Harcus and the ladies at the Red Cross shop at Avalon Beach.

My deep appreciation goes to the academics whose meticulous research on seemingly mundane issues such as housework and gender roles tells the true story of the massive social upheaval we're going through. The prolific output of researchers like Lyn Craig and Barbara Pocock contributed enormously to the content of this book. On the cooking side, I am indebted to Vickie Smith, whose book *Miss Vickie's Big Book of Pressure Cooking* continues to be my bible.

My delightful colleagues at the ABC, who make going to work such a pleasure, have given me recipes, advice and plenty of belly laughs when needed most. The talented stylists of the ABC's make-up department all deserve medals, not only for turning me from frumpy housewife to glamorous news presenter every day, but for the hour and a half of counselling and friendship they throw in for free.

Finally, my heartfelt thanks and love to Mario Milostic, my co-creator not only of this book, but of the two amazing little humans who are our proudest achievement, Marcus and Mischa.

contents

intro *page* 3

01 **life** *page* 11 / living the dream page 13 / oh baby, what a nightmare *page* 17 /
the nanny-go-round *page* 19 / fairy grandmothers *page* 25 / the slippery slope *page* 26 /
crunch time *page* 27 /

02 **food** *page* 35 / fast food nation *page* 37 / help! I forgot to get takeaway *page* 39 /
pressure. and cooking *page* 42 / pressure. and money *page* 43 / survival cooking *page* 44 /
what you need *page* 48 / stocking the pantry *page* 49 / grocery shopping *page* 53 /
confessions of a bad mother *page* 55 / the cubist movement *page* 57 / recipes *page* 59

03 **time** *page* 75 / time squeezing *page* 79 / time shifting *page* 81 / time blocking *page* 83 /
hidden time *page* 85 / being organised *page* 88 / keep it simple *page* 93

04 **home** *page* 99 / hey guys, want more sex? *page* 101 / the great domestic
divide *page* 103 / a bit of history *page* 111 / technology versus reality *page* 124 /
secrets of a desperate housewife *page* 125 / chore wars *page* 130

05 **family** *page* 137 / the good old, bad old days *page* 144 / the birth of
superwoman *page* 144 / which brings us back to role reversal … *page* 149 / so why do it? *page* 150 /
surviving the work/family juggle *page* 158 / the big question *page* 161 / now … *page* 162

06 **pressure cooking** *page* 167 / pressure cooking FAQs *page* 168 /
the pressure cooker story *page* 177 / the australian love affair with pressure cookers *page* 178 /
how to use a pressure cooker *page* 181 / safety checklist *page* 187 / advanced pressure
cooking *page* 189 / learn from my mistakes *page* 189 /

07 **recipes** *page* 197 / first things first: stock *page* 202 / soups and side
dishes *page* 206 / rice and pasta *page* 216 / main meals *page* 224 / desserts *page* 246

endnotes *page* 254

Today's families are going through the biggest social changes in modern history – a revolution in the way we work, live and raise our children. We can see these changes as catastrophic, or we can see them as an opportunity to create something better, a world in which 'work/life balance' is a reality, not just a catchphrase. But getting there is tougher than many of us ever imagined. We can look to the past for some solutions and the rest we just have to figure out for ourselves. There are no rules or roadmap. We are the new pioneers.

intro

AT WHAT POINT DID OUR LIVES become so ridiculously busy?

As I write, Australians are working the longest hours in the developed world. We spend much of our life stuck in traffic or commuting. Even with both spouses working, record numbers of families have lost their homes in recent years, hit by years of high inflation and interest rate rises, then KO'ed by the global financial crisis. More than half of all workers say they are struggling to get by. Obesity and depression are at epidemic levels.

We're so stressed we don't even have time for that most basic survival need: feeding ourselves properly. So we buy takeaway. Or we zap something frozen in the microwave. And guess what? Our kids are the first generation to have a good chance of dying before us, from diseases related to poor diet. Australia has become a nation of fat, sad, exhausted people.

What is happening to us? How on earth did we end up in this mess – and what can we do to change it?

have a
nice cup
of tea, a
Bex and
a good
lie down.

Advice given to
stressed Australian
housewives in the
1950s

Life seemed a whole lot easier last century. Growing up in Brisbane in the 1970s, I remember long hot summers that seemed to last for years; entire months spent wandering around the neighbourhood, barefoot, looking for something to do. Dad went out to work, Mum was at home. A few people had a flash new thing called Bankcard, but mostly they paid cash. Dinner was meat 'n' three veg, with tinned fruit and cream for pudding. Our time after school was our own, to play in the streets and backyards of our suburb, while Mum and Dad had their 5.30 pm sherry on the patio. Home computers and the internet were years away. Everything happened ... slowly.

Nobody pretends it was perfect. After all, several generations of housewives were addicted to Bex and Vincents, and after that they got stuck into the valium. But whatever the drawbacks, life was simple and predictable. It was manageable. Above all, life back then had the one thing that today we crave so desperately: time.

These days, life is so busy that 'free time' is like some quaint historical notion that disappeared with twin-tub washing machines. Even our children don't get the chance to be bored – the moment they stop, we rush them off to another themed birthday party, baby Pilates or a weekend seminar for gifted children.

As for the adults, it's no longer enough to just do your job and look after your family. Popular culture dictates that we should also (in no particular order) have a beautiful home, exercise three times a week, meditate for 20 minutes a day, be up-to-date on news and current affairs, floss, download songs onto our iPods, raise funds for our children's school, recycle, wear designer clothes, look after our ageing parents, get our teeth checked every six months, study for an MBA, schedule romantic 'dates' with our spouse, see the latest movies/bands/art exhibitions and – my personal favourite – drink two litres of water a day. (Have you ever tried that? You spend most of the day running to the loo – it's a part-time job!)

Somehow, we've been hoodwinked into thinking we can do it all. The fact is, it's a rort. If we try to meet all these ridiculous expectations, we'll crack. I should know – I had the glamorous job, the gorgeous family and the big house with water views – and I still ended up having a very public collapse in front of half a million TV viewers (which continues to be enjoyed by an international audience on YouTube).

In nearly 30 years as a journalist, I have seen work/life balance become one of the biggest social and political issues of our age. Some aspect of it makes the news every day – whether it's the debate over paid maternity leave, unions pushing for more flexible working hours, or a high-profile person quitting to spend more time with their family. There's a wealth of academic research that tracks how quickly our lives are changing as governments struggle to come up with policies that reflect the new reality.

But the most important voices in this social revolution are largely silent. There are very few personal accounts coming from the front line, from the people who are actually experiencing 'the juggle'. It's no mystery why. Like soldiers in the thick of battle, they just don't have the time to send a postcard. If they did, it would probably contain just one word – 'Help!'

This book evolved, in part, from a cover story I did for *The Bulletin* magazine in January 2007. Written from a personal perspective, it looked at the increasingly devastating impact of the work/life juggle on Australian families. Although different from the magazine's usual political fare, the story drew a huge response. Emails and letters poured in. It was picked up by talkback radio. Behind Australia's affluent, aspirational suburban facade, there seemed to be a well of frustration, even desperation. People bailed me up at the local shops and in the corridors at work, speaking about their own struggle to balance the demands of modern life. They weren't looking for solutions; they just seemed relieved that someone had taken an interest.

You can find thousands of books that tell you how to micro-manage every conceivable aspect of your life, from relationships to career to having a baby and cooking healthy meals. But, as I found, there's nothing that tells you how you're meant to do it all simultaneously.

So that's how this book happened. Half journal, half cookbook, it's basically a collection of postcards from the work/family battlefront, written in 15-minute bursts between kids and work and cooking, and all the usual domestic crises, like moving house and children's birthday parties. I don't claim to have the answer to getting control of your life in this frantic age we live in. I certainly don't claim to represent families in general – while we all have much in common, everybody's circumstances are different. All I can tell you is what worked for me after I crashed and burned.

And it all started with something I stumbled upon in an op shop. Something, oddly enough, I recognised from growing up in the 1970s: an old Hawkins pressure cooker.

Despite the widespread

acknowledgement that managing

work and family is an issue

of profound and growing

importance, surprisingly little is known about

the full extent of the challenges

involved and whom

they most affect.

Social Policy Research Centre report, 2008 [1]

life is like
a box of
chocolates.
you never
know what
you're
gonna get.

Forrest Gump

life

It felt like we were in a long-running series of Survivor. Once we'd completed the challenges the smiling host would appear, shouting 'Congratulations! You've got your old life back!' But gradually it dawned on me – nobody was coming. There was no rescue helicopter on its way. This was our life now. The old one was gone.

life

I LOVE OP SHOPS. When I was a kid I used to scour them for Enid Blyton books. Then, in my teens, it was all about vintage fashions like winklepickers and fake leopard-skin coats. Once I had children, I discovered them all over again. With a toddler and a baby to entertain, the local op shop became a regular haunt. On rainy days, the kids could raid the toy-boxes while I read old bestsellers – without getting the death stares we'd attract at the library or the toy shop.

Frankly, though, the kids were just an excuse. To me, an op shop is an Aladdin's cave full of treasure. Everything in there has a story. There's the same lady behind the counter in every single op shop in the Western world – she's called Joyce, she's in her 70s, and she has glasses and permed grey hair. But in all my years of cruising op shops in all corners of the globe, this was the first time I'd ever seen a pressure cooker.

It was obviously vintage, but in mint condition, and it came with the original instruction booklet. Whoever donated this cooker had loved it enough to carefully wrap the booklet in plastic. Inside, there were bad colour photos of a perfect 1970s family, seated at the dinner table being served by a smiling woman with back-combed hair. 'In today's world where you are faced with too much to do, and too little time or money to do it, pressure cooking has become a necessity!' cried the blurb inside.

I paid Joyce and hurried home excitedly. Like the blurb said, I had too much to do and too little time to do it in. I'd just made the papers for all the wrong reasons – a spectacular death-by-choking impression during the 7 pm news. Things were not looking brilliant. It was the first time I'd ever considered an old pressure cooker might have the answer; but then, life often presents you with opportunities when you need them most. Sometimes they come in very strange forms, you just have to recognise them. Right then, I needed an opportunity to change my life. And what better place to find it than in an opportunity shop?

Living The Dream

If someone had told me five years previously I'd be getting excited about a pressure cooker, I'd have said they were insane. Back then, I was living in London, working as a news anchor for CNN International and living a very glamorous single life indeed. Eating meant eating out – usually at the latest fashionable restaurant in Notting Hill. My fridge contained vodka, fresh limes and pre-packaged frozen meals in case of emergencies. A girls' weekend away meant flying to Istanbul and sunbathing on a boat in the Black Sea. If I felt like some new clothes, I'd catch the Eurostar first class to Paris to go shopping. At work, I'd be interviewing Shimon Peres one minute and Gerry Adams the next. World leaders and film stars could be found wandering the corridors with their entourages, asking how to get to

Opposite page: Beryl Wales and Bonny at the Red Cross Shop, Avalon Beach.

the studio. I carried my passport in my handbag in case I had to go abroad at short notice. 'Katie's called in sick,' the boss would say apologetically. 'Would you mind going to Venice/Warsaw/Paris for a couple of days to do the arts program?'

Outside working hours, CNN parties were packed with diplomats, dissidents, war correspondents and the occasional spy. It was a fabulous, exciting and utterly ridiculous life.

The downside was getting up at 1.30 am, five days a week, to be prepped and ready to go on air at 5.30 am. Plus, it was lonely – my friends were often on assignment overseas for months at a time and the unsocial hours were a major barrier to any kind of personal life. After five years, I packed up and came home to Australia in search of normality, a nice boyfriend and a good night's sleep.

Mario and I met almost as soon as I arrived back in Sydney, in a café around the corner from the flat I'd rented. He'd also spent a lot of time overseas – first as a professional tennis player, then as a graphic designer working in New York and London. During his six years on the international tennis circuit, he enjoyed all the perks that a young handsome sportsman on the loose can expect – and a few that came as a complete surprise, like meeting Brigitte Bardot in a Parisian nightclub, drinking vodka shots with Yannick Noah in Toulouse and ending up at Rod Stewart's birthday party after a big night out in London. When he retired from tennis he followed his other passion – art – and became a highly regarded graphic designer and art director. When I met him, he was living the glorious life of a popular bachelor in a stylish harbourside apartment that he'd renovated himself.

Six weeks after we met, we got engaged on a deserted beach. It was sunrise. A pod of dolphins was swimming past. Life was very, very sweet. And then? Well, then we got married and had two babies within two years. I'd heard about reality. Occasionally, I'd even stepped in it – but I'd always managed to scrape it off my shoe and get back to the carefree fantasy that passed for my life up until that point. And here I was, up to my neck in it, along with this handsome stranger I'd known for about five minutes who looked every bit as shell-shocked as I was.

Oh Baby, What a Nightmare

Like most new parents, we had no idea how much our life was going to change once we had kids. In fact, we'd never even changed a nappy before. We figured that life would continue pretty much as normal, only better.

So before the baby arrived, we bought a large, rundown house on Sydney's northern beaches, an hour from the city. It was the peak of the housing boom, so we stretched ourselves to the limit financially to get it. But why not? We had two incomes, didn't we? Yes, it would be a long drive to work and back but hey, it's a small price to pay for the view and the lifestyle, right? The house was 40 years old and needed complete renovation, but we figured we'd do that ourselves, on the weekends, while our baby slept happily in his cot.

Yeah, right.

About five minutes after we bought the house, Sydney's housing boom abruptly ended. Interest rates started to storm upwards and property values began a steady slide south. Our baby arrived – not via the peaceful water birth we had meticulously planned but after a traumatic labour followed by an emergency caesarean.

Back home, it turned out that caring for a baby was very different from the picture painted by celebrity mums in women's magazines. We were expecting love, joy and a feeling of completion. Instead, we felt a rising sense of panic and overwhelming exhaustion. For the first few months, I got an average of three hours' broken sleep a night, rising to between four and five hours for the next couple of years.

(Sleep deprivation, incidentally, was an approved torture technique used by US interrogators at Guantanamo Bay. The official guidelines stated that the tortured detainee must be allowed four consecutive hours sleep every 24 hours – considerably more than a lot of new parents get!)

I was so dazed in the early weeks that once I completely forgot I'd even had a baby. I was upstairs when I heard a strange yowling sound.

'Must be a tomcat outside,' I thought absently, picking up the laundry basket. 'Funny how they sound like babies crying. Oh … it IS a baby crying. Quite nearby, too. What's a baby doing inside my house … oh shit, it's MY baby!'

According to the baby books, a good mother is able to identify her child's cry in the midst of a hundred wailing infants. It took me a full 30 seconds to distinguish mine from a tomcat – that's how good I was.

When Marcus was 12 weeks old and still being breastfed, I went back to full-time work as the ABC's 7 pm news presenter. It was summer, which meant I was also presenting a late-night news bulletin, finishing around 11 pm. By the time I got home to my hungry son, it was after midnight, and I was like an over-inflated Zeppelin about to explode.

The only place at work to express milk was the toilets, so I'd perch on the loo in between news updates and use a plastic breast pump. As pleased as I was to be back at work, it also felt sad and demeaning to be sitting on the toilet collecting my breastmilk in a plastic container, when I really wanted to be nursing my baby, 50 kilometres away.

Expressing takes ages, so it was a good opportunity to think. There is a custom in more traditional parts of the world where women stay in bed for 40 days after the birth of a child. Freed of domestic work, all they have to do is lie there, feed the baby and recover from childbirth.

When my husband was born in 1965, his mother's village in Croatia still observed the custom. She tells a wonderful story of how she lay in bed for 40 days, nursing her son, while her mother and the other women of the village took turns cooking, cleaning and admiring the baby. At the crack of dawn on day 41, her mother marched into the room, whipped off the bedcovers and said, 'OK, enough! Time's up, my girl – there's washing to be done!'

In Australia, I thought we seemed to have gone to the other extreme – a casual indifference to the physical demands of childbirth and motherhood that sometimes, unintentionally, borders on the brutal. It wasn't so much that a nursing mother recovering from major surgery would be put straight onto the full-time late shift, it was that nobody – including me – had thought twice about it. Years later, when I told one of my managers what a struggle it had been, she was mortified. 'It honestly never occurred to us,' she admitted.

In any case, within a week of going back to work, my milk suddenly dried up. So that was one less dilemma to deal with.

The Nanny-Go-Round

If the reality of working motherhood seemed harsh, I knew I was one of the lucky ones. I had agreeable bosses, 12 weeks' maternity leave, and a well-paid job I loved. If I was the privileged end of the working-mother spectrum, I wondered, how on earth were the others doing it?

It quickly became apparent that it was impossible for both Mario and me to continue with our full-time careers as well as care for our new baby. For financial reasons, we decided I would continue to work full-time while he accepted a part-time lecturer's position at a design college in the city. This would allow him to also freelance from home and look after Marcus while I was at work. It sounded like the ideal solution but, of course, it didn't quite work out that way. Mario's new part-time jobs quickly became more full-time than before, and it was obvious we needed outside help.

Being a journalist, I was fully informed about the childcare crisis. But somehow it had slipped my mind while we were house hunting. Naturally, we had chosen to live in an area where the nearest under-2 childcare facility was a 20 minute drive away. Oh, and it had a 2-year waiting list, of course.

Thus began our bumpy ride on the nanny-go-round. We had sexy, vague Tiffany, who was a brilliant nanny but always rang in sick on Monday morning after a hard weekend of clubbing. Whenever she failed to turn up, our day would be thrown into complete chaos. All plans would have to be cancelled and rescheduled, and there'd be a desperate ring-around of relatives to see if anyone could help.

Then, when our second baby arrived, we had Juliet, who was the perfect nanny – too perfect. I depended on her so much that when she quit to take care of her terminally ill mother, I cried for three days.

I used to dread putting the Help Wanted ad in. The phone would ring non-stop for a week. There'd be women who had no experience with babies ('I thought I'd give nannying a go! How much are you paying?'), women who couldn't speak a word of English and women who sounded keen but never showed up for the interview. On two occasions, we hired girls who then texted us the night before they were due to start, saying they'd had a better offer.

Like most families, we were forced to use 'black market' nannies – paid cash in hand, tax-free – because agency nannies were simply unaffordable. (One colleague was paying $50 000 a year – almost his entire after-tax income – to cover his nanny's wages, super, holiday and sick pay. While he was regarded by the government as an 'employer', with all the associated costs, he was unable to claim any of it back on tax as a work expense.) I recognise that caring for our precious children should be well paid – but it galled me that it was so scarce and so expensive that we had to break the law every time we hired a nanny.

Finding childcare was without a doubt the biggest stress of those early years. When the second nanny in two weeks sacked us by SMS, I rang Mario in tears, totally distraught.

'Forget the nanny, it's all too hard,' he said. 'Our life is being dictated by strangers who couldn't care less. Let's do it ourselves.'

'Are you mad?' I sobbed. 'There's no way we can do it alone.'

But surprisingly, there was.

Mario quit his college job and became a full-time at-home dad. Until 2 pm each day he would work in his studio on freelance design projects while I looked after the house and the kids. Then we'd swap, and I'd head in to work. Now that our lives no longer depended on a third party it felt like a huge weight had been lifted. To my astonishment, life without a nanny actually became less stressful.

Nonetheless, with two very young children and our jobs to manage, it was still frenetic. The worst part was the domestic chaos. Life at home could be summed up in three words: Cleaning Up Mess. I'd tidy up, then five minutes later it would look like the house had been ransacked by robbers. If I took two minutes to check my emails, I'd return to find the toddler had emptied a bag of sugar onto the floor – and the baby eating it by the handful. The laundry, cooking, cleaning and grocery shopping was never-ending. And it all had to be done while simultaneously feeding, changing and supervising two small domestic terrrorists. We were going through so many disposable nappies we had to order an extra garbage bin from the council.

As much as I adored my children, I was shocked, dismayed and

Gives them a *whiteness* that makes y... *proud*

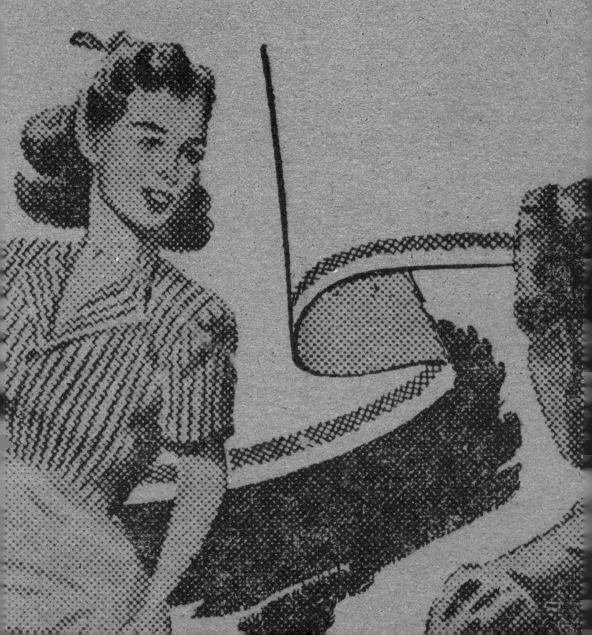

horrified at the wholesale destruction that motherhood itself had wrought on my life. According to the women's magazines which occasionally interviewed me, I was blissfully happy and had, in their words, the 'perfect life'. I was intrigued to read about this parallel universe where, apparently, I was effortlessly combining career, marriage and babies. In the magazine world, I even looked a lot better, with my blemishes and crow's feet air-brushed out, and a wardrobe of designer clothes provided by the magazines just for the photo shoot.

In the real world, though, I was tired and grumpy. I was discovering what mother-of-four Antonia Kidman would later describe as the 'code of silence' surrounding motherhood. 'Most of us put on a brave face, keep up appearances,' she would write for *Sunday Life* magazine. 'It's only when things fall apart that the truth comes out.' [2]

At that stage, my life was still a few months away from falling apart. I was deep in denial, waiting impatiently for our old life to suddenly re-materialise. It felt like we were in a long-running series of *Survivor*. To win, we just had to get through the sleep deprivation, the childcare crises, the endless mess and the all-night stints at the emergency department. Once we'd completed the challenges the smiling host would appear, shouting 'Congratulations! You've got your old life back! And you get to keep the kids, too!'

But gradually it dawned on me – nobody was coming. There was no rescue helicopter on its way to get us off Hellfire Island. This was our life now. The old one was gone – and we would never get it back.

The day this finally sank in, I didn't get depressed. I just got really angry. When I couldn't find my car keys due to the general household chaos, I up-ended my handbag with a furious shriek, jumped on it several times, then kicked it clear across the room with an almighty karate yell. Mario said it was the most hilarious yet terrifying display he'd ever witnessed. Then I went to work and calmly read the news.

Fairy Grandmothers

Kicking the handbag was a turning point. Once I accepted the loss of my old life, things improved. Surrendering to chaos delivered a wonderful gift: gratitude. I was grateful simply to have two healthy children. I was grateful for the rare night that wasn't interrupted by nosebleeds, night terrors or a trip to the local hospital. I was grateful for sunny days so the children could play outside. Going for a walk on my own was like winning the lottery. Five hours of sleep in a row was my highest goal in life. In short, I started to appreciate the important things in life. To my surprise, shopping in Paris was no longer one of them.

I was particularly grateful to have both the children's grandmothers alive, healthy and happy to help. Mario's mother Marija was our rock, our port in a storm, our bridge over troubled waters. I marvelled at her ability to calmly control multiple grandchildren at the same time as cooking dinner and running up a sofa cover on her sewing machine.

When we sent out a distress call, Marija always answered. On the days I had no time to feed myself, I knew I could always call into Marija's on the way to work for a bowl of chicken soup and a 15-minute nap on her bed. She'd send me on my way with a food parcel for the next day. When Marija visited us, she always managed to discreetly clean our entire house before she left. The old me would have been mortified. But now, humbled by the thousands of small indignities inflicted by motherhood, I just hugged her and whispered, 'Thank you'.

My own mother, at 80, did not have Marija's extraordinary energy, but she had time and patience, and she loved to play. After making the long trip by train and bus from Newcastle, she would spend hours rocking and singing a fretful baby to sleep while we passed out. The children adored their Grandma and Baba, and we simply couldn't have coped without them.

The Slippery Slope

Financially, though, things were looking disastrous. Rising interest rates and exorbitant childcare costs had wiped us out. We suddenly found ourselves part of Australia's newest social class – the wealthy poor – people with good incomes and big houses who couldn't afford to get their teeth fixed.

Like the panicking crew of a sinking ship we started off-loading assets, tossing them overboard like deck chairs in the hope of staying afloat. One by one we sold the properties we had brought into the marriage. Mario sold his beloved BMW convertible and, with gritted teeth, bought a $7 000 Commodore. But it still wasn't enough. Every time the preschool fees were due I'd sell a piece of furniture on eBay. The luxury trappings of our pampered single lives were disappearing faster than our joie de vivre.

The process made me realise how much 'stuff' we had. Oddly enough, getting rid of stuff felt good. The less stuff we had, the lighter we felt. It was an interesting concept, and I filed it for future consideration.

With interest rates rising virtually every month, the obvious solution was to sell the house, but first we had to make it liveable so that somebody would buy it. With no money for tradesmen, the only option was for Mario to do the whole job himself. He had very little experience, but loads of determination. I realised that the day a truck dumped 12 tonnes of sandstone boulders on the driveway. I was aghast.

'How in God's name are you going to move them? They're massive!'

'I'm not sure yet,' he said thoughtfully. 'I guess I'll buy something at the hardware store to cut them up into smaller pieces.'

Incredibly, within a few weeks he'd turned the boulders into a series of beautiful sandstone retaining walls. In the same way, drawing on his design skills, he taught himself basic building, plastering and landscaping.

Fixing the house had become Mario's full-time occupation through sheer necessity, but he was still looking after the kids when I went to work, then doing freelance design jobs once they were in bed. Meanwhile, I took on a second job to cover the interest rate rises – writing a column for *The Bulletin* magazine. I'd get home from the ABC at 10.30 pm, write my column until 1 or 2 am, then grab a few hours sleep before the kids woke up at 6 am.

My workload was now verging on impossible but I couldn't bring myself to let go of that second job. Writing was my selfish little treat. It was the only thing I had left that was just for me – but it also turned out to be the final straw.

Crunch Time

Several months later, I woke in the middle of the night with excruciating chest pain. Every breath was like being stabbed. My first thought was: heart attack. But as stupid as it sounds, I didn't have the energy to get the whole family out of bed to go sit in an understaffed emergency ward. I lay quietly and took shallow breaths until the pain subsided. When I finally got around to having a chest x-ray two weeks later, I was diagnosed with pneumonia.

The drugs helped but I was left with a persistent cough and shortness of breath. Reluctantly, I gave up *The Bulletin* job, but it didn't make much difference. I continued to numbly look after the children, run the household and cough my way through news bulletins. Mario and I would see each other for about five minutes a day, at 2 pm 'handover' time.

I felt like I was slowly drowning.

One morning, confronted by the perfect storm – crying baby, raging toddler and a mountain of dirty dishes – I locked myself in the toilet and crouched on the floor, gasping for breath. The local GP diagnosed asthma and prescribed a puffer.

It didn't help.

I became convinced I was dying of some rare terminal illness and lay awake for hours at night worrying about how Mario and the kids would cope. In between secret bouts of weeping I organised my will and life insurance and Googled my symptoms on the internet to identify what I was dying from. The diagnosis was instant and surprising – hundreds of pages titled 'panic/anxiety disorder'.

Work became my refuge. It was the only place I got to rest. I suddenly understood how generations of male breadwinners had felt – the blessed relief of driving away from a chaotic household and a faint ambivalence about returning to my loved ones when work was over. Mario, meanwhile, was experiencing the downside of being at home full-time with very young children – boredom and isolation. 'Stay a bit longer,' he'd say as I rushed out the door just a little too eagerly. 'Once you're gone, I'll only have the kids to talk to …'

The ABC newsroom, despite the pressure of deadlines and late-breaking news, was a haven of calm and predictability compared to what awaited me at home. I could focus on a single task and complete it without constant interruptions. Nobody followed me into the toilet demanding to know what I was doing. The make-up artists diligently covered up my cold-sores and black circles and the studio crew even brought me a cup of tea before I read the news. Every night, I thanked them profusely and told them I looked forward to that cup of tea all day. It was our little joke – except I wasn't joking.

Grateful for the respite, I made a big effort to maintain my cheery, professional facade, pretending that nothing had changed since the birth of my children and that life continued as normal. But it was getting harder. I was telling more and more fibs to cover the fact that

I hadn't read a newspaper or watched *Lateline* in months, that I didn't have a clue what was going on in the world and – worst of all – that I didn't really care.

One night, I opened my mouth to introduce the night's top story – and nothing came out. I tried to clear my throat. Still nothing. As I croaked and whispered my way through the lead story, I could hear the stunned murmuring in the control room through my earpiece. 'What's going on? Is she all right? Get Deb Rice into make-up – NOW!'

In between stories I was bent double with coughing, trying to clear my throat. The floor manager, Stuart, belted my back and fetched glasses of water. By now, it wasn't just my voice that wouldn't work – I was also struggling for air.

I later found out I'd probably had a 'laryngeal spasm' due to the stress of the situation. In simple terms, my vocal cords closed up so I couldn't speak or breathe. More commonly, it's the body's response to drowning. It was one of those golden spontaneous moments of television – 'a panic attack, captured live on air!'

The studio director switched to the Melbourne bulletin while I calmed down. I went back on air 10 minutes later with a smile, apologising for our 'technical difficulties' and joking that a cough lolly and a glass of water had sorted them out. But inside I was shocked and frightened. I'd finally heard the wake-up call.

That night, over several strong margaritas, Mario and I committed to making some radical changes. We weren't sure exactly what they would be, but we knew they had to happen fast. Our life was totally out of control. It was eating us alive.

We knew that whatever it took, we wanted a simpler life. A healthier, quieter life, with a lot less stuff in it. The kind of life, in fact, that we remembered from our childhood.

Times had changed, of course. The pressures on families these days were enormous – and they were about to get worse. Mortgage rates were peaking at record levels and petrol was about to hit nearly $2 a litre. Just around the corner was the global financial crisis, the worst since the Great Depression. Within 12 months, world markets would collapse, plunging the whole country into fear and uncertainty.

But that was all ahead of us. Right then, all we knew was that something had to change. We knew we couldn't control interest rates or the number of childcare places. But we could control how we managed our lives given those circumstances. We could make decisions about the way we worked, the way we raised our kids, how we spent our time and money and the kind of house we lived in.

And we could start with the most basic and yet the most important choice of all – what we ate.

Mario's relatives celebrate food and family in the village of Blato, on the Croatian island of Korcula in the 1960s. The courtyard of the old stone house, which has been in the family for centuries, is still where friends and relatives gather today.

Families are rarely sitting down together for a meal, and when they do it's usually later than ever before, as longer working hours and other commitments battle for our time. [3]

and when they do, its usually later than ever before

families are rarely sitting down together for a

own together for a meal, and when they do it's usually later than ever

down together for a meal, and when they

families are rarely sitting

king battle for our time

before as longer wor

hours and other com

it is in
the preparation
of the dinner
that the cook
begins to feel
the weight and
responsibility
of her situation.

Mrs Beeton's Book of Household Management, 1861

food

The day my six-month-old son arrived home from Baba's with garlic breath I knew it was all over. At an age when the World Health Organisation reckoned he should still be exclusively breast-fed, he'd been happily eating Baba's pasta. Confronted with the evidence, she admitted he'd been getting his gums around a lot of other food too. 'He loves it. He's a good eater,' she said proudly.

food

A FRIEND RECENTLY HAD HER KITCHEN RENOVATED. The centrepiece of it, and her pride and joy, was a gigantic stainless-steel European stove with six gas hobs and multiple ovens.

'But you never cook,' I pointed out.

'I know. But I'm going to learn,' she said. 'Really! As soon as I get some time.'

This gorgeous, expensive spaceship of a stove was so complicated my friend had to do a half-day course, offered by the stove company, just to learn how to operate it. That's right – you can do a course. About a stove. Needless to say, my friend is still trying to find some time in her busy life to actually cook something on it.

It reminds me of the glossy cookbooks I've got stashed in every corner. I buy them, flick through them and fantasise about the meals I'm going to cook and the dinner parties I'm going to host. And then I go and make spag bol for the 200th time.

There's something very, very weird about our relationship with food these days. We're obsessed by it. We read about it, we watch programs about it on TV, but we don't actually 'do' food all that well.

'Families are rarely sitting down together for a meal, and when they do it's usually later than ever before, as longer working hours and other commitments battle for our time,' the *Daily Telegraph* reported after a recent study on the issue.

People eat microwaved dinners in front of the TV or at their desk at work. Fat kids make themselves instant noodles while they play computer games and wait for their equally fat parents to get home with takeaway (62 per cent of adult Australians are now overweight or obese).[4] We look at books full of recipes we never make and buy expensive kitchen appliances we never use. The wealthiest countries in the world cannot stop the morbidly obese eating themselves to death, or anorexics starving themselves.

Fast Food Nation

I only realised quite how weird it had all become when I met my husband. In his culture, food rules. It's one of the most important and pleasurable parts of life. When Mario's parents emigrated to Australia from Croatia in the 1960s, they brought with them the fabulous cuisine of their island home. A combination of Italian and Balkan influences, it involved a lot of pasta, seafood and rich stews (or 'wog food' as the Aussies charmingly referred to it back then).

'My friends would come over and say, "What? You eat barbecued octopus?!"' Mario remembers. 'Then they'd try it. After that, they'd be back the next day for more!'

Croatian women are amazing cooks. If you turn your back on my mother-in-law for five minutes she'll whip up a quick feast of baked squid stuffed with savoury rice, or a platter of palacinkas, paper-thin pancakes rolled around smoked salmon.

37

'It's nothing. Just a little something. Very light,' she'll say with a shrug. 'Please – eat!'

There's always a pot of soup simmering on her stove, a tray of pastries about to come out of the oven and a bunch of home-grown spinach that somebody has dropped off as a gift. It's like Harrod's food hall.

The men are into cooking, too. Mario's uncle, Mladen, goes fishing in Pittwater then barbecues his catch and invites the rest of the family around for a seafood banquet. The barbecue is actually a small brick hut, complete with tiled roof and chimney, modelled on a Croatian konoba, or smokehouse. Forget about those tin plates on skinny legs we grew up cooking snags on, that's not a barbecue. Baba Mladen's konoba, now that's a barbecue!

Humans have always regarded food not just as a basic survival need, but as a celebration of family and community. Regardless of race, religion and economic status, eating together is one of the most satisfying and joyful aspects of the human experience.

But somewhere in the past couple of decades, we've lost that. We've become disconnected from food to the point where fewer and fewer people even cook their own food, let alone grow it or catch it. That's why we buy the expensive stove and the glossy cookbooks. We yearn for good food and the life it represents. We want it back. Our separation from it causes all sorts of horrible illnesses and plays a big part in the sickness and sadness of modern society.

The culprit, yet again, is lack of time. 'Fast food' is a reality of modern life, but in fact it's an oxymoron. Good food is not fast. A meal takes time. You have to plan it, buy the food, transport it home, store it, prepare the ingredients, cook it, serve it, clean it up, and get rid of the waste and packaging. And then, when you've done all that, it's time to start thinking about the next meal …

For me, the biggest single challenge of the whole work/family juggle – the mother of all issues – has been food.

Help! I Forgot to Get Takeaway!

The preparation of food only became a critical issue for me once I got married and had children. Suddenly, I no longer had only myself to think about. I had to plan ahead; I had to be organised. I was A Mother, with all the guilt and expectation that entails. A bowl of cereal at 11 pm was not an acceptable dinner for young children, or for a large hungry husband who'd been doing heavy renovation work all day. I had to learn to cook.

The other catalyst was shift work. In television news, 'normal' working hours involve random combinations of early mornings, late nights, public holidays and weekends. News is a 24/7 business which means that anyone who works in the industry becomes accustomed to organising their own meals to eat at their desk. They have three options: takeaway, pre-packaged supermarket meals or home-cooked meals.

The tiresome thing about being a TV presenter is that a diet of takeaway, however convenient, is definitely not on – you have to keep yourself nice, after all. Staying off the Thai chilli beef and pizza is mandatory in a cut-throat industry that does not favour the obese. In my single life, work meals consisted mainly of what I dubbed Mean Cuisine – pre-packaged meals that claimed to be the 'healthy' option. They came in plastic sachets that needed to be nuked in the microwave to the point where they blew up like puffer fish and threatened to explode. The chief reason they kept you lean was the tiny portions, barely enough to sustain a grasshopper.

At CNN, organising an evening meal was not an issue because I worked early mornings. But the problem cropped up again when

crazy modern food solution number 1

A few months ago I caught up with an old flatmate, Simon. In our single days, he'd been a trim and cultured bloke who cooked a healthy meal for himself every night, accompanied by a cheeky glass of fine wine. Naturally, he was snapped up by the first woman who realised he wasn't gay. After he married and had kids, he really porked up, and that was the last time I'd seen him. But when we met again, I was astonished to see he'd lost a huge amount of weight and was looking fantastic. Knowing that both he and his wife had insanely busy executive jobs, I quizzed him about the cooking issue.

'The nanny shops and cooks for the kids, and Karen and I have been on Trim 'n' Simple for the past two years,' he told me. 'Initially we did it to lose weight. Then it was just so convenient, having these meals delivered every week. So we're on it permanently. Neither of us is in any mood to cook when we get home from work around 8 or 9 pm. It takes the pressure off knowing there's always a ready-made meal in the freezer that we just stick in the microwave.'

The cost? Expensive. Up to $170 per person, per week.

crazy modern food solution

number 2

Luke and Sylvia have high-pressure jobs in the corporate world and two teenage children. Both of them are extremely stressed, but need two incomes to pay the mortgage and school fees. Their work is so demanding that usually neither of them is home before 8 pm, and they're often on call. Over the years, they've stacked on a lot of weight and both have experienced health problems as a result. Sylvia had been a terrific cook in her 20s and hosted many a dinner party. So when I asked her what the family ate these days and who cooked it, the answer surprised me.

'We eat takeaway five nights a week,' she said. 'The kids get to choose – Chinese, Thai, pizza, whatever. Luke or I pick it up on the way home.' Wasn't she concerned about the weight and health aspect? 'I know. I feel terrible about it. The thing is, I'm happy to cook a couple of nights a week, as long as Luke does the same. But he absolutely refuses. He says he doesn't have the time to buy groceries or cook, even once a week. So I cook on the weekend and we get takeaway during the week. That's our compromise.'

The cost? A staggering $300 a week.

I started working nights at the ABC. By that stage, I was well and truly over the plastic sachets and determined to stick to healthy home-cooked meals as much as possible.

Pressure. And Cooking

Then the babies started arriving. In the beginning of my juggling act, cooking healthy meals for a family seemed logistically impossible. At one point, I was preparing a separate meal for each person: mashing vegetables for the baby, adding some poached chicken for the toddler, cooking an adult meal for my husband, and putting yesterday's leftovers in a plastic container to take to work for myself.

The cycle of cooking was relentless. However much I prepared, my family devoured it like locusts, then looked around hungrily for more. Food was the first thing I thought of in the morning ('Oh God! What can I make for dinner today?') and the last thing at night ('Damn! I forgot to take the meat out of the freezer for tomorrow'). As the children grew, their dietary needs and whims changed almost weekly, complicating things even further.

I tried shortcuts: buying prepared pastas and salads from the local shops, and hitting on the two grandmothers to send emergency food parcels for the babies. But no sooner was one meal sorted than I had to start thinking about the next. The logistics of providing three healthy meals per day for four people were staggering. Mrs Beeton was right: I was feeling the full weight and responsibility of the situation.

So, by the time I discovered the pressure cooker in the op shop I was desperate for a long-term solution. And the old Hawkins, bless it, turned out to be exactly what I was looking for.

Most people remember pressure cookers from their childhoods – they were popular here from the 1940s right through to the 1970s (and in Europe and Asia, they've never gone out of style). But even though they're considered a bit old-fashioned, the truth is, there is no method of cooking more suited to the hectic pace of today's lifestyle.

A pressure cooker works on a very simple principle. It's basically a large pot with a lid that locks on and seals airtight. The steam builds up inside and has nowhere to escape, so the pressure, and consequently the temperature, start to rise. Under full pressure, the food is cooked at a very high temperature – which cuts the cooking time by around two thirds. The steam keeps things moist and tender, and the sealed environment locks in the nutrients. It's simple, healthy – and very very fast. (See chapter 6 for an introduction to pressure cooking and basic recipes.)

The old Hawkins opened up a whole new world to me. Once I got the hang of pressure cooking I invested in a large, modern cooker with all the bells and whistles. Soon, I could turn out several days' worth of meals in 45 minutes. I discovered that by using the pressure cooker – and by freezing large quantities of whatever I made – I was able to put healthy, tasty meals on the table at fairly short notice. For the first time since having kids, I felt the panic subsiding. I was actually getting something under control. I had a system!

Pressure. And Money

Thrift is back in fashion thanks to the global financial crisis – and the pressure cooker is a great way to save money as well as time. Quite apart from the cost benefits of cooking in bulk, pressure cooking uses much less energy because it is so fast. A third of the cooking time means using a third of the energy – good for the planet as well as your wallet.

Coincidentally, pressure cookers first became popular during another period of enforced frugality: the lean years after WWII. At a time when good-quality food was expensive and hard to come by, pressure cookers became an essential household item. Australian housewives soon found that pressure cooking was a great way to save money because it allowed them to use the cheapest cuts of meat. (Under full pressure, even tough meat is tenderised by the super-heated steam.) Indeed, when my parents married in 1948, their first major investment was Mum's cast aluminium pressure cooker – the one she's still using today, 60 years later.

Survival Cooking

Before you read on, you need to know something. I'm not a great cook. Before I had kids, I could barely cook an egg. These days, through sheer necessity, I've upped my standard to average. I have a limited repertoire of tasty meals that my family seems to like. I'm an expert at soups, casseroles, salads, pasta and toasted sandwiches – quick, easy stuff I can knock up before I have to go to work. Pressure cooking accounts for probably 50 per cent of my output – it's the only way I've found to cook lots of food, very quickly.

The recipes in this book are nothing special. In fact, you may have your own versions of them already that you know off by heart. But the reason they're in this book is that these are the recipes that work for me – a full-time working mother with four people to feed, and a job that means I'm never at home on week nights. These are the meals I feed to my family. They're do-able, seven days a week. Even better, they can be made in bulk and frozen for later use.

Like most parents, I want my kids to have a healthy diet, and to the best of my ability within the circumstances, I cook with that in mind. In an ideal world I would love to use home-grown organic produce, make my stock from scratch and have a pantry without a single tin in it. But I know from experience, as a full-time working mother, that it's logistically impossible to do that. I take shortcuts – using tinned tomatoes, minced garlic in a tube, lemon juice in a bottle, ready-made liquid stock and curry paste – because time-wise, there is no other option.

There are several cookbooks on the market that go into the whole science of pressure cooking. This isn't one of them. The purpose of this chapter is to introduce you to a system of cooking that enables you to provide your family with healthy, home-cooked meals every day – even when you are working full-time and have no domestic help. It's a system I've developed through trial and lots of error. It's not perfect and it's not very pretty, but it will get you through. I call it Survival Cooking.

Survival cooking is a simple way for busy people to produce large quantities of healthy, home-cooked food so that they never have to buy takeaway. It is ideally suited for families in which both parents work either full-time or part-time, but it's also handy for singles who work long hours, go out a lot and are concerned about their diet. It's perfect for mothers with babies or toddlers who don't have the time to cook every day, but don't want to feed their children from jars or tins. And it's great for dads who are taking on more of the domestic duties and need a basic introduction to family cooking.

There are five main elements:

- cooking in bulk
- cooking very quickly, usually in a pressure cooker
- using a small number of simple recipes
- using basic ingredients and lots of fresh vegetables
- freezing portions for later use

The first thing you have to accept with cooking is it takes time. Not necessarily a huge amount of time, but more time than buying a takeaway. Using a pressure cooker cuts cooking time to around one third, but you still have to plan your meals, shop for groceries and prepare the ingredients.

Once you accept this, you need to somehow find that time. This requires another old-fashioned concept: sacrifice. Something will have to give. Maybe it means letting the laundry pile up a bit higher before you get round to doing it. Maybe you cancel your weekly yoga class, or postpone visiting a friend, or give up your favourite TV program so you can use that hour to cook. Yep, it hurts. I know. But if you want a healthy diet, it's got to be done. (In chapter 3, I'll talk about the techniques of time squeezing and time shifting which also help.)

The other thing we've come to expect with our food is endless choice and variation. Survival cooking, by contrast, is basic and repetitive. Fewer choices mean fewer decisions to make, and that's the whole point of it: anything else is simply not realistic for an excessively busy person. The more variety you have, the more complex and time-consuming cooking becomes.

That's not to discourage you from trying new things when you've got the time. But if you're really busy, it's just too hard. Survival cooking lets you off the hook because you know that in a crisis you've got a limited number of simple recipes that work. The principle of 'cook in bulk, then freeze' also limits the choice, because not everything is suitable for freezing.

As a result, you'll find yourself perfecting a repertoire of about a dozen meals that you can whip up in 20 minutes, confident that your family will eat them without complaint. I make an awful lot of chicken schnitzel, for example. Mainly so I can hear my three-year-old daughter try to say 'schnitzel'. But also because I can make a huge batch of it, then freeze it, and I know it's always going to be a hit.

So you get the idea: survival cooking is very plain. You'll notice that in many of my recipes, I tend to throw a whole lot of ingredients in together and cook them at the same time, rather than staggering the cooking times, or using separate pots. It's not very elegant, but it's fast – and that's what counts. The aim is not to impress everyone with your stylish cuisine. You're not out to win a Michelin star for amazing dinner parties. You can do that later. Right now, your main priority is to cook nutritious meals for your family in the shortest possible time, with the least amount of stress and washing up. This part of your life won't last forever, so let go of your expectations. There'll be time enough to mix your own curry spices and grow organic basil when you've retired.

Survival cooking is often a haphazard affair; you need to be flexible. There's a lot of improvising, because lack of time means the pantry often doesn't contain the exact ingredients you need. No paprika to add to your goulash? No worries. Leave it out, and you've got stroganoff. No tinned tomatoes for your bolognese? Cut up some fresh ones, open a bottle of pasta sauce, or mix some water with tomato paste. Personally, I'm not a fan of the American habit of using tinned soup as a substitute for making your own sauces – but if it works for you, go for it. It certainly saves time.

If you're stuck for a key ingredient, you can often save a dish by adding chilli sauce, Dijon mustard, soy sauce, Worcestershire sauce, coconut milk, or some other condiment that changes it to something completely different. I once complimented my mother-in-law on a fantastic spicy beef stew, which I assumed had Eastern European origins.

'What's in this sauce? Paprika? Fresh chillies?' I asked, preparing to write down a complicated recipe.

She went to the fridge and pulled out a jar of vindaloo curry paste.

'One tablespoon of this – and a bottle of pasta sauce,' she said.

Remember: limited choice is good. You don't have to think as much. When you're a Survival Cook, mince will become your good friend. Don't fight it. You'll discover that however you dress them up, most meals come down to meat 'n' three veg. You'll discover that as long as you've got an onion and a tin of diced tomatoes, you're halfway there. You'll discover that if your kids eat pureed spinach and chilli beans three nights in a row, it won't kill them. They'll survive. And so will you. That's what survival cooking is all about.

What You Need

1   *Pressure cooker.* This brilliant appliance is the basis of survival cooking and, of course, the whole point of this book! (See chapter 6 for information on how much they cost and where to buy them, along with basic instructions on how to use one.) However, if you want to take things slowly (quite literally) all the recipes here can also be made in a regular, large pot. They'll just take two to three times as long. Obviously you can still cook in bulk and freeze in portions, regardless of whether you use a pressure cooker or a regular pot.

2   *Stick blender or food processor.* I use a good-quality blending wand, which has lasted for five years and has a small food processor it can be attached to for larger chopping jobs. I prefer that to a full-size food processor because it is quick to assemble and clean, and takes up much less storage space.

3   *Ice-cube trays.* Go for the ones that are divided into larger sections, not smaller (they tend to be messy when you're spooning puree into them). The ideal size is big enough to fit a tablespoon of blended food without it spilling over the sides.

4   *Freezer bags or plastic containers* for storing the frozen cubes. And if you're really diligent, labels for dating them.

5   *Extra freezer, if possible.* This is not essential but if you get serious about cooking in bulk, you'll need the extra space. A chest freezer is ideal, but even an extra fridge/freezer is handy.

Stocking the Pantry

Survival cooking uses a basic, versatile range of ingredients, topped up with whatever fresh fruit and vegetables are in season. These are the staples I always have in the kitchen.

*   beef and chicken stock (liquid)
*   coconut milk
*   couscous
*   curry powder
*   Dijon mustard
*   dried pasta (including angel hair for noodle soup)
*   flour (for thickening stews and sauces)
*   grated cheese (kept in the freezer)
*   minced garlic (in a jar or tube)
*   rice
*   tinned corn
*   tinned three-bean mix
*   tinned tomatoes (plain)
*   tinned tomatoes (with added basil and herbs)
*   tinned tuna

Tip

THE THRIFTY COOK buys a large jar of generic tomato paste, then freezes it in an ice-cube tray, one dessertspoon per portion. When frozen, remove cubes and store in a plastic bag in the freezer so you always have some on hand.

Eat your vegies or I'll put the wooden spoon around your backside!
Of all the wisdom our parents passed on to us, this is probably the most practical and timeless (except for the wooden spoon bit, which these days would lead to criminal charges).

Fresh vegetables are a really important part of survival cooking because they're healthy and they're easy. They're the perfect 'fast food' for our busy modern lifestyle. Regardless of what you're cooking, it takes very little time to peel and slice a few vegetables and throw them in. And if you've got fussy children, vegetables are easy to disguise. You just blend them with whatever else you're cooking (either by pureeing or grating) and they take on that flavour.

The key to freezing vegies is not to overcook them first. Greens in particular should only be partly cooked, then, when they're thawed and microwaved, they're still firm and tasty. You can tell you've got it right if the vegies are still bright and colourful when you eat them.

It's not like the old days when Australian housewives used to boil vegetables to the point where you couldn't recognise them. When I first started cooking my own meals I was astonished to find that steamed broccoli was actually bright emerald green as opposed to army khaki.

Tip

THE CLEVER COOK runs cold water over green vegetables for 10 seconds after steaming or boiling them. It stops the cooking process and keeps them bright green.

Although most of the recipes in this book use a pressure cooker, I prefer to use a regular pot or saucepan to steam vegetables. The reason is that all vegetables take slightly different lengths of time to cook perfectly, and with a saucepan, you can just take off the lid at various stages and throw in the next lot of vegies. (I always do all my vegies in the one pot to save time.) I also like to regularly poke a fork into the potatoes and carrots to test when they're done.

With a pressure cooker, it's just too much trouble to be de-pressurising and re-pressurising every time you want to add or check something. Some people swear by pressure cookers for doing their vegies, and people who are expert at it have elaborate stacking systems for cooking all the separate parts of a meal simultaneously. But my advice is, cook your vegetables in a separate saucepan at the same time as you're making the other part of the meal in the pressure cooker.

Grocery shopping

Busy people don't have the luxury of popping out to the shops whenever they run out of something, so one of the keys to successful survival cooking is shopping efficiently. The aim is to keep your kitchen stocked well enough that you don't run out of things, but not so well that food goes off and you have to throw it out.

Like most household chores, grocery shopping is not brain surgery, but there is a technique to it. When you're buying large amounts of fresh fruit and vegetables, there's a surprising amount of logistics involved, and doing it properly involves forward planning and good organisation. Meat can be frozen and non-perishables keep for ages, but with fresh fruit 'n' veg, there really are no shortcuts with time – you just have to go to the shops to buy them, probably twice a week.

You can buy frozen vegetables (just as nutritious as fresh, surprisingly), but if you've got to buy fruit anyway, you may as well pick up fresh vegetables as well. Internet shopping is one option, but I never used it for fruit and vegetables because somebody else is choosing the produce for you, and if you're not at home when it arrives, it sits in the sun for hours, wilting.

Fruit and veg apart, there are ways to save time on food shopping and cut down the number of trips you do.

- *Buy in bulk.* This is one area where internet grocery shopping works really well. You can buy all your bulky, heavy, generic items (bottled things, toilet paper, nappies, laundry detergent, tinned food, etc) online once a month and have them delivered. If you stick to non-perishable stuff, it doesn't matter whether you're there to receive the delivery or not, as long as it's left somewhere safe. I'd never suggest that you save time by doing your internet shopping while you're at work. Of course not. But I've heard that some bad people find it very helpful.

- *Have a separate fridge/freezer* for storing bulk goods like meat and bread. When the kids were little, we quickly discovered the perils of running out of milk at 10.30 pm. So with both kids drinking huge quantities of milk, I used to buy three 3-litre containers at a time and store them in my husband's old bachelor fridge in the garage. Then I found the freezer was good for storing six loaves of bread and several trays of meat. Once I established the system, I found I could do one large shopping trip per week, with one or two smaller runs to top up the fruit and veg.

- *Have a shopping list handy* in the kitchen to write down things the moment you run out of them. Otherwise – you WILL forget, and you WILL end up making an extra trip, and you WILL end up buying stuff you don't need. Trust me on this. Busy people need a shopping list (even my husband, who once declared that 'shopping lists are for people with weak brains'). However, be aware that the only shopping list that will last longer than a day is the sort that has the pen permanently attached to it; one that you can put on the fridge or the wall, out of reach of little hands.

- *Shop late at night.* This is the shift worker's secret. Most big supermarkets are open until midnight but after about 9 pm there are very few shoppers – and lots of things on special. I often buy the groceries late at night on my way home from work because it takes about a third of the time it takes with children in tow. It saves you time, money and stress. It might mean you lose 30 minutes sleep – but it'll save you a ghastly two hours battling the Saturday morning supermarket crush.

Confessions of a Bad Mother

I tried hard to feed my children processed baby food, I really did. Yes, I know – Bad Mummy! Processed baby food is nasty stuff. I knew that. But here's the thing: by the time Marcus was starting solids, I was back at work full-time. I was worn out trying to get the hang of a new baby, as well as run the house, commute two hours a day, and still be a productive employee. Cooking every day for a baby as well as for two adults seemed logistically impossible, and I knew he couldn't live on mashed bananas forever.

So I decided to pay a visit to the dark side. At the supermarket I looked at the towering shelves of jars and tins plastered with colourful pictures of smiling babies and thought, how bad could it be? They sell tons of this stuff! Some of it's ORGANIC, for crying out loud. It'll just be for emergencies, not for every meal. Look, that one's got couscous in it – that's healthy. C'mon! Besides, I have to leave for work in 20 minutes.

I threw a dozen tins and jars into the trolley, feeling dreadful. Processed food was so not the way I'd planned to go, but I didn't see any other realistic option. Later, I opened a jar of Gourmet Organic Roast Pumpkin with Couscous and tried to feed the gluey orange contents to my son. He spat it out. I tried again. He turned his head and squealed angrily. I tasted it, in case it was off. It tasted like – nothing. I couldn't detect a hint of either pumpkin or couscous. I gave up and mashed a banana for him.

The next day, determined to try again, I went to the pantry to select a jar. The shelf was empty. The whole lot had disappeared. I searched the kitchen and found them in the rubbish bin.

'Why did you throw the baby food away?' I asked my husband through gritted teeth.

'Because the lids are coated with a cancer-causing chemical,' he replied calmly. 'You announced it on the news last night – remember? I thought maybe it's best we don't feed it to our son.'

That stopped Bad Mummy in her tracks. For a second.

'Well ... they're not ALL cancer causing,' I argued. 'Just the ones with the lids that go pop when you open them. Everything else is perfectly safe. Anyway, I have to leave for work in 20 minutes.'

I'm not proud of what happened next. I'm actually embarrassed to admit it. But the minute Mario went back to his studio I tiptoed to the rubbish bin and very quietly retrieved a tin of processed baby food (the non-carcinogenic variety) and tried to coax my son into trying it. He wouldn't have a bar of that one, either.

It was no mystery why, really. My mother and mother-in-law had completely ruined my baby for processed food by feeding him a tempting array of fresh pureed vegetables and fruit from the earliest possible opportunity. The official guidelines at the time stated that a baby should not start solids until the age of six months. The two grandmothers scoffed at this. The day Marcus turned four months old there was virtually a stampede to get the first spoonful of real food into his mouth.

He took to it like a professional, much to the delight of his Baba

Marija. In true European style, she could not rest until a child had consumed so much he was about to pop. Watching her spoon avocado into his bulging cheeks reminded me of the exploding fat man in the Monty Python sketch trying to cram just one more thing in.

'A wafer-thin mint, monsieur?'

KABOOM!

The day my six-month-old son arrived home from Baba's with garlic breath I knew it was all over. At an age when the World Health Organization reckoned he should still be exclusively breastfed, he'd been happily eating Baba's pasta. Confronted with the evidence, she admitted he'd been getting his gums around a lot of other food too.

'He loves it. He's a good eater,' she said proudly.

There was no turning back. My baby was hooked on the good stuff. I realised then there would be no shortcuts to feeding him a delicious, healthy array of meals. I just had to figure out how.

The Cubist Movement

The idea of cooking up large quantities of baby food, blending it, then freezing it in ice-cube trays had never occurred to me. Too busy to join a mother's group or read baby books, I lived in the isolated world of the full-time working mother, trying to figure out solutions to problems I'd never encountered before with little information.

But when I stumbled on frozen baby food cubes at the supermarket, the penny dropped. Here, it seemed, was the perfect solution: baby food made from fresh ingredients, with no additives. But the supermarket cubes were bland, and very expensive. I decided I could do a better job myself.

My first attempt at making my own frozen cubes – a traditional Croatian spinach and potato dish – was so successful that before long I was turning out more than a dozen varieties of pureed fruit and vegetables, soups and smoothies. Armed with a hand blender and a few ice-cube trays I could create a fortnight's worth of meals for the baby in a couple of hours.

No matter how busy Mario and I were, we could just grab a selection of cubes from the freezer and have a healthy meal for the baby within minutes. A typical meal might be cauliflower cheese with spinach and zucchini, followed by a mango yoghurt smoothie for dessert. Or, in the colour code of frozen cubes – two white, one green, and two pale orange.

A few tips:
- To puree the food, you can use a food processor or a blending wand. I prefer the blending wand for speed and convenience – there's less to wash up, and you can puree the food in the pot it's cooked in.
- To release the frozen cubes from the ice-cube tray, run hot water over the bottom.
- Store the cubes in freezer bags or plastic containers and, if you're a goody two-shoes who actually has the time, label and date them.
- Go easy when adding butter. Young babies also shouldn't have any salt at all.

Baby steps: Survival Cooking 101

The following are some of my favourite recipes for fast, healthy baby food, most of which can be pureed, then frozen in cubes. Some of them are also suitable for pressure cooking, but for the sake of consistency, all the instructions are for the regular cooking method.

Once you've got the hang of the bulk blending and freezing technique you may wish to start using the pressure cooker where appropriate. (See chapter 6 for an introduction to pressure cooking.)

Note: Babies need to be introduced to solid food in stages, so see your GP or local early childhood centre for advice on the right time to start your baby on certain foods.

Baby Chicken Stock

This clear liquid is the basis for many of the first solid meals your baby will eat. It adds a delicate flavour and also contains nutrients from the vegetables that are cooked with it. Chicken stock is used in a whole range of recipes suitable for all ages, so if you've never made it, now's the time to start!

While it may seem like a hassle, it's actually very easy. It freezes really well too, which means you've got it on hand whenever you need it – a much cheaper, healthier alternative to buying processed stock.

Pressure cooking time: 20 minutes
Regular cooking time: 90 minutes

RECIPE INGREDIENTS

1 roast chicken carcass (or 750g chicken neck bones, available at supermarkets) / 2 litres water / 1 onion / 1 carrot / 1 tomato / 1 stalk celery / 2 cloves garlic, whole

Put all ingredients into a large pot and bring to the boil. Simmer for 90 minutes (or 20 minutes in a pressure cooker). Strain liquid into a bowl and allow to cool. Discard the other ingredients. Refrigerate the stock for a couple of hours and then skim off any fat from the surface. Pour into several plastic containers and freeze for future use.

Tip

THE CLEVER COOK can also whip up a quick clear broth using a couple of chicken breasts or thighs if no bones are on hand. Add a potato or other vegetables to the pot and as well as your clear broth, you'll end up with some tasty poached chicken meat and vegetables for yourself or a toddler. This can also be pureed for older babies.

Victorian Association of Day Nurseries and Creches

DAY NURSERY OR CRECHE

ADDRESS

DAY BOOK

Closed on Public Holidays

Although most Australian mothers stayed at home in the 1950s, there were creches available for those who worked for pay. This 'day book' from 1952 was filled out by the nursing sister in charge of the babies, recording each child's daily eating, sleeping and toilet regime in fine detail.

'The sister wrote down everything your baby ate during the day, when they slept, and when they had a bowel movement. The mother filled in the other side of the book, so the sister could keep an eye on how you were looking after them at home. It was a very strict routine in those days. You fed your newborns, for example, every three hours round the clock – at 12, 3, 6 and 9. Not a minute sooner, not a minute later. If they were crying for a feed and it wasn't time – well, they just had to wait. If they were asleep, you woke them up. And do you know what? Babies in those days learnt very quickly. I never had any trouble with my babies not sleeping through the night. They had a dirty nappy at the same time every day. It was very easy to toilet train them because of that.'

Gaye Phillips, mother of four

PARENT

DATE	EVENING MEAL	HOURS OF SLEEP	BREAKFAST	BOWELS	REMARKS
27-3-'52	Boiled Egg, Toast, Milk	7PM - 6.30AM.	Rolled Oats, Toast, Milk	7.45 AM	
28-3-'52	Sandwiches, Banana, Milk	7PM - 6AM.	Puffed Rice, Toast, Milk	7.15 AM.	
31-3-'52	Toast, Banana, Milk	7PM - 6.30AM	Rolled Oats, Toast, Milk	7.15 A.M.	
1-4-'52	Scrambled Egg, Toast, Milk.	7PM - 6AM	Puffed Rice, Toast, Milk	7.15 AM.	
2-4-'52	Sandwiches, Banana, Milk.	7PM - 6.30AM.	Rolled Oats, Toast, Milk	7.45 AM.	

62

DINNER	SLEEP	BOWELS	REMARKS
Liver, potato, beans, pumpkin	12·30 — 2·0		
Apple sponge & milk			
milk, apple			
Mince steak potato	12·15 — 1·45	✓	
marrow, cabbage			
pears & junket			
milk, apple			
Tripe, potato,	12·20 — 1·30		
parsley, carrot			
pears & rice			
milk, pear			
Steak, potato, beans	12·13 — 1·30		
pumpkin			
Stewed apple & ground rice			
milk, pear			

In 1952, Australia was still a British outpost, a country that referred to lunch as 'dinner'. Dr Spock, with his more relaxed attitude to raising babies, was a decade away. The creche day book records in detail what my eldest sister was eating for breakfast (rolled oats, toast, milk), for 'dinner' (lambs fry, marrow, beans, stewed rhubarb and junket) and in the evening (boiled egg, toast, banana, milk). She slept between 12.15 and 1.30 every day, give or take five minutes. Modern-day 'baby whisperers' advocate a similarly strict regime.

Baby Beef Stock

Pressure cooking time: 20 minutes

Regular cooking time: 2 hours

RECIPE INGREDIENTS

2 tbsp olive oil / 500 g beef bones (or cheap cut of meat like chuck or casserole steak, cut into cubes) / 1 onion, roughly chopped / 1 stalk celery, roughly chopped / 1 carrot, roughly chopped / 2 litres water

Pour the oil into a baking tray. Toss the meat and vegetables in it until lightly coated, then bake in a hot oven (200°C) for 20 minutes or until brown. Pour off any excess oil, then put all the ingredients into a large pot with the water and simmer on the stove top for 2 hours (or 20 minutes in a pressure cooker). Strain liquid into a bowl and allow to cool. Discard the other ingredients. Refrigerate the stock for a couple of hours, then skim off any fat from the surface. Divide into plastic containers and freeze for later use.

Tip

THE SAFE COOK knows stock must only be frozen and thawed ONCE during the process of making a meal. Too much re-freezing and thawing allows bacteria to breed. So, if you are using defrosted stock in a recipe, the meal must be eaten immediately, or refrigerated and eaten within a couple of days. The alternative is to make the stock, refrigerate it, then use it within a couple of days to make a bulk meal, which can then be frozen.

Spinach and Potato

This is a Croatian version of a universal favourite, with the olive oil adding a wonderful flavour. It makes a delicious side dish for adult meals too – just add a little salt and, instead of blending it, mix roughly with a fork until the potato breaks into small 1 cm lumps. It took me ages to get the proportion of spinach to potato right – I kept putting too much potato in, which makes it very bland. So go heavy on the spinach and be generous with the olive oil. The finished cubes should be a lovely rich, dark green.

Pressure cooking time: 10 minutes

Regular cooking time: 20 minutes

RECIPE INGREDIENTS

2 medium potatoes, peeled and quartered / 4 bunches English spinach, roughly chopped / ½ cup olive oil / (Optional: add a chopped zucchini or a handful of chopped beans)

Boil potatoes in a large pot until almost soft. (If you are using the beans or zucchini, put them in after 10 minutes.) Meanwhile, wash spinach and cut stalks off. Once the potatoes have been on for about 15 minutes, place handfuls of the spinach into the boiling water. Press down with the lid. (Spinach wilts and reduces in size quickly as it cooks, so you should be able to get the whole lot in within a couple of minutes.) Cook for 5 minutes, until both potatoes and spinach are soft. Drain, add the olive oil and puree. Allow to cool. Freeze in ice-cube trays, then bag and label.

Pumpkin, Carrot and Sweet Potato

These bright orange cubes have a lovely sweet flavour that makes them perfect for young children. The sweet potato adds a bit of starchiness to the mix, which is otherwise a bit sloppy. Be careful not to add too much though, or it becomes too stiff. You can adjust the ratio of pumpkin to carrot depending on taste and what you have in the fridge.

Pressure cooking time: 7 minutes

Regular cooking time: 20 minutes

1 small pumpkin, cut into small pieces (Jap or Queensland Blue are best) / 4 carrots, sliced / 1 small sweet potato or ½ a larger one, sliced / 1 tbsp butter / ½ cup milk (or formula)

Boil the vegetables for 20 minutes (or 7 minutes in a pressure cooker). Drain, add butter and milk, then blend. Freeze in ice-cube trays, then bag and label.

Creamy Chicken Casserole (Puree)

This recipe uses a poached chicken breast, but you can also use leftover barbecue chicken pieces, without the skin.
Regular cooking time: 20 minutes

RECIPE INGREDIENTS

2 cups chicken stock (see recipe on page 59 or use ready-made low-salt liquid stock) / 1 chicken breast / 1 tbsp olive oil / 1 onion, chopped or grated / 1 small potato, chopped or grated / 1 carrot, chopped or grated / 6 button mushrooms, chopped / 1 tbsp flour / 4 tbsp milk (or formula) / ½ cup grated cheese

Bring a cup of stock to the boil in a saucepan. Add chicken breast and simmer for 5 minutes or until cooked through. Remove chicken and allow to cool. Chop into small pieces. In a separate pan, heat the oil and cook the onion, potato and carrot on medium heat for 5 minutes. Add mushrooms and cook for a further 3 minutes, stirring occasionally. Add flour and stir for another 2 minutes. Slowly pour in the remaining stock and milk and bring to the boil. Lower the heat, add the chicken pieces, and cook for 5 minutes. Remove from the heat and stir in cheese until melted. Allow to cool. Puree and freeze in ice-cube trays.

Beef Casserole (Puree)
Pressure cooking time: 10 minutes
Regular cooking time: 30 minutes

RECIPE INGREDIENTS
200 g fillet steak, finely diced / ½ cup flour / 1 tbsp olive oil /
2 cups beef stock (see recipe on page 65 or use ready-made low-salt
liquid stock) / 1 potato, finely chopped / 1 carrot, finely chopped /
1 zucchini, finely chopped / 6 button mushrooms, finely chopped /
2 tbsp tomato paste

Put the meat and flour into a plastic bag and shake to coat. Heat the
oil in a pan and brown the meat on both sides. Slowly add the stock,
scraping the crusty brown bits off the bottom of the pan as you do
(this is called deglazing, and adds a lovely flavour). Add the vegetables
and tomato paste and simmer on medium heat for 30 minutes, stirring
occasionally. Allow to cool, then puree and freeze.

Fish with Cheese and Vegetable Sauce
Regular cooking time: 25 minutes

RECIPE INGREDIENTS
1 tbsp olive oil / 1 onion, chopped / 1 stick celery, chopped /
1 carrot, grated / 1 potato, chopped into small cubes / ½ cup broccoli
florets, peas or other green vegetable / 1 fillet of white, flaky fish
(whiting is good) / 2 tbsp butter / 1 tbsp flour / 2 cups milk / ½ cup
grated cheese

Heat the olive oil in a pan and sauté the onion, celery and carrot for
about 3 minutes or until soft. Add potato, broccoli and enough water

to cover, then boil for 10 minutes. Add the fish fillet and simmer for another 5 minutes. Drain and set aside. To prepare the cheese sauce, in a separate pan, melt the butter, add the flour and stir to a thick paste. Gradually add the milk, whisking constantly until it forms a thick sauce. Add cheese and stir until it melts. Combine fish, vegetables and cheese sauce. Puree and freeze. For toddlers, skip the blending and leave it chunky.

Tuna Pasta Bake

This has always been a fast, reliable stand-by in our family, and enjoyed by both kids and adults. For babies, use small pasta shapes.
Regular cooking time: 30 minutes

RECIPE INGREDIENTS
2 cups pasta spirals / 50 g salt-reduced butter / 1 large onion, chopped finely / 1 tsp crushed garlic / 50 g plain flour / 1½ cups of milk / 1 cup grated cheese / 425 g tin tuna, drained and flaked / 1 cup frozen peas or small pieces of broccoli / 125 g tin of corn kernels

Preheat the oven to 180°C. Lightly grease a small baking dish. Put the pasta on to boil while you prepare the cheese and tuna sauce. Heat the butter in a large saucepan and sauté onions and garlic for 3 minutes. Stir in flour and cook for another 5 minutes. Add a splash of the milk and continue to stir until the sauce thickens, then gradually add the rest of the milk, stirring constantly. (If the sauce refuses to thicken, you might need to increase the heat.) Add half the cheese, tuna, peas and corn, and stir until cheese has melted. Combine the pasta and sauce in the baking dish and sprinkle remaining cheese over the top. Bake for 20 minutes. Serve as is for toddlers and adults; puree for babies and freeze in portions.

Mango Strawberry Smoothie

There are dozens of different fruit combinations you can puree and freeze to make a healthy sweet treat for your baby. This is just one of them, and the possibilities are limited only by your imagination (and what fruit is in season). Fruit has enough natural sugar in it, so don't add any extra. This age is also a good time for your baby to get used to the taste of natural yoghurt.

RECIPE INGREDIENTS
2 mangoes / 1 punnet strawberries / small tub natural yoghurt

Cut the fruit into pieces, then puree to a smooth mix. Add the yoghurt, stir, and freeze in small containers or ice-cube trays.

Stewed Apple and Rhubarb

One of my earliest food memories is eating Mum's stewed apple and rhubarb and I've continued the tradition with my own kids. The key to successful stewing is to use only a small amount of water (there's plenty in the fruit already) – you'll have to fight your natural inclination to add more than you need. Even as they get older, children love it with a bit of sweet yoghurt or custard. Alternative combinations include apple and pear, apple and apricot, and apricot and peaches (when in season).

Pressure cooking time: 5 minutes
Regular cooking time: 15 minutes

RECIPE INGREDIENTS
1 cup water / ¼ cup sugar / 4 granny smith apples, peeled and chopped / 1 bunch of rhubarb, cut into pieces about 3 cm long

Bring the water to the boil and stir in the sugar until it dissolves. Add the fruit and simmer over a low heat for 15 minutes. Drain off any excess water, blend, and freeze in ice-cube tray.

THE FRUGAL COOK buys bulk lots of overripe or slightly damaged fruit when it is on special. Stewing fruit does not need to be perfect and fruit markets often sell off their excess or seconds stock very cheaply.

Apricot Porridge

Once you've got your frozen fruit cubes, they can be used in all sorts of ways, as well as on their own. This is a quick way to make your baby's breakfast a bit more interesting. For younger babies, you can substitute formula and rice porridge for the milk and oats combo.

Regular cooking time: 5 minutes

RECIPE INGREDIENTS
½ cup one-minute oats / 1 cup milk (or formula) / 3 frozen stewed apricot cubes (prepared as above) or other pureed fruit (tinned is fine, at a stretch)

Combine the oats and milk in a saucepan and bring to the boil. Reduce the heat and stir in the defrosted cubes. Cook for 1 minute, stirring constantly, until porridge thickens.

Meal plannin

Bíc

WITH *Balanced Flavour*

...nced Flavour ! A subtle blend of matured
...a zestful tang to tickle the palate of any
...s to delight m'lady . . . a creaminess that
... more ! Balanced Flavour—the secret of

and trim chops, peel and slice onion. Place
epan with mint, parsley, lemon rind, water,
e celery leaves, salt, and pepper. Cover and
1¼ hours. Remove lemon rind, mint, and
Add diced celery, simmer further 45 minutes.
off all but ¾ cup of the liquid, preserving it
in gravy, etc. Blend flour smoothly with milk,
pan, stir until boiling. Simmer 2 or 3 minutes.
ping hot, sprinkled with finely chopped celery

BED CUTLETS WITH SAVORY SAUCE

: One dessertspoon fat, 1 onion, 1 table-
our, ½ pint water, 1 dessertspoon Worcester-
uce, 1 tablespoon vinegar, 4 or 5 peppercorns,
tspoon red currant jelly, ½ teaspoon salt.
at, add diced onion, cook until lightly browned.
ur and brown. Stir in water, sauce, vinegar,
orns. simmer while preparing and cooking
When required for serving, strain
jelly and salt, and re-heat.
s: Six cutlets, 1 tablespoon
tablespoon milk, crumbs

utlets in flour, pepper
milk. Toss in crum
ife-blade. Brown
heat and cook
es. Drain on

ed an attract
ual quantities
iled egg-whit
ogether.

ECONO

nd a half cu
gg, 1¼ cups n
hopped chive
bacon), 1 dess
tripe, place in
Bring to boil,
dd 1 teaspoon s
1½ to 2 hours o
mincer. Sift flou
, mixing to a smoo
of finely chopped onio
ut of butter in small p
n kitchen paper. Melt a
2 full tablespoons of tripe mi
with spoon. Cook over steady
lightly browned underneath. Loosen edges,
wn, and set other side. Lift on to hot plate,
while balance cooks. Use a little more butter
flapjack. Serve hot with grilled tomato

ECONOMY MUTTON HOT-POT

d a half pounds neck of mutton, 1 dessert-
t, 1 onion, 1 tablespoon flour, 1 pint water
½ teaspoon meat extract, ½ teaspoon salt, pinch
tablespoon barley (or 2 tablespoons barley
1 large green apple, piece of swede, 1 carrot,
oon chopped parsley.
ll meat from bones, discard fat and gristle,
into small pieces. Brown lightly in hot fat,
d onion and flour and brown. Add stock,
tract, salt, pepper, washed barley (or dry
ernels), diced apple, swede, carrot. Cover
ner very gently 2 to 2½ hours. Just before
old in chopped parsley.

ECONOMY POT ROAST

edium-sized shin of beef, 4 rashers fat bacon,
oons flour, ½ teaspoon pepper, ½ teaspoon

Place the two pieces of meat together and tie or ske
firmly. Mix flour, pepper, salt, nutmeg, cloves, m
tard, and brown sugar. Rub thoroughly into m
Melt fat in heavy saucepan, add meat, brown well
all sides. Add water and vinegar, cover closely, c
2 to 2¼ hours, turning meat occasionally. Add wh
onions and halved carrots. Continue cooking with
on until vegetables are soft—about 30 to 40 minu
Lift meat and vegetables on to hot serving-d
thicken gravy slightly, and serve in a gravy-b
Serves approximately five people.

LAMB AND CORN CASSEROLE

Six lamb chump chops, 1 dessertspoon fat, 3 sr
onions, 1 cup sweet corn, 1 cup diced celery, ¾
hot water, ½ cup tomato puree, ¼ teaspoon meat
tract, 4 small potatoes, salt and pepper to ta
chopped parsley.
Trim chops, removing all fat. Brown lightly
es in melted fat, place in casserole. Fill
layers of sliced onion, corn, cel
with salt and pepper. Mix n
and tomato puree. Pour ca
peeled, sliced potatoes on
derate oven (350deg. F.
2 hours. Remove lid,
s brown.

FF
lt and caye
cooked lam
tablespoon chop
rboiled red pepper
eadcrumbs, 1 dess
lespoon grated ch

parsnips, season w
and sides of grea
xture. Combine m
ite sauce. Turn
eadcrumbs mixed v
d cheese. Bake in
25deg. F. electric) 2
hly heated and lig
ith tomato slices and p

OPS MEXICANA

1 onion, 1 dessertspoon fa
tablespoons vinegar, 1½ cups st
olespoon Worcestershire sauce, 1
brown sugar, 2 tablespoons chutney, 1
diced celery, 1 teaspoon salt.
Trim all fat from chops, brown lightly on both s
in hot fat; remove. Add sliced onion, allow to bro
lightly. Stir in flour, cook 2 or 3 minutes to bro
Add vinegar, stock or water, sauce, sugar; stir u
boiling. Return chops to pan, add celery, chutn
and salt. Turn into casserole, cover, bake in mo
ate oven (350deg. F. gas, 400deg. F. electric) 1½ t
hours, until chops are tender. Serve hot, garnis
with parsley.

HOT CHICKEN TIMBALE

One and a half cups minced cooked poultry,
cooked macaroni or spaghetti, 2oz. diced ham, 1
soft breadcrumbs, salt and cayenne pepper to tast
teaspoon finely minced onion, pinch grated nutr
¼ pint milk, 2 eggs, 1 tablespoon melted margarin
butter, parsley.
Grease a plain pudding-mould thickly, line bot
and sides with cooked, drained macaroni or spagh
Combine poultry, ham, breadcrumbs, salt, pep
onion, nutmeg. Mix with beaten eggs, melted short
ing, and milk. Allow to stand 10 to 15 minutes
turning carefully into prepared mould. Cover

all my
possessions
for a
moment
of time.

Elizabeth I

time

People juggling work and young families in particular find the sheer number of competing demands overwhelming. Instilling some sense of order and predictability into an otherwise chaotic environment is the only way you'll get through those challenging years with your physical and mental health intact.

time

THAT'S ALL VERY WELL and thanks for the recipes, I hear you say. But who has the time to cook, even if it is with a pressure cooker? Who has the time to do anything these days?

Of course you're busy. But you're reading this book, aren't you? That means you've already employed some form of time management, allowing you to prioritise this book above all your other pressing concerns.

My guess is that you've either 'shifted' or 'squeezed' your daily allotment of time to fit it in. You may also have 'sacrificed' or even 'stolen' time to read this book. (Yes, that means you, the one reading it under your desk at work. Don't feel guilty. How do you think I found the time to write it?)

There's an old saying: if you want something done, give it to a busy person. That's because busy people are extremely efficient at using every available minute in the day. They're good at changing their schedules at short notice to fit in extra, unexpected tasks. They're brilliant at squeezing, shifting, sacrificing and stealing time so they can do it all.

That's why the juggling metaphor has become part of our everyday language. The single word 'juggle' needs no explanation. It's become short hand for the staggering number of tasks that many of us do simultaneously.

Personally, I prefer the term 'spinning plates'. While a juggler at least gets to stand in one spot, the circus performer who spins plates on top of thin canes is in constant motion. As soon as he gets one plate spinning, he darts off to catch another before it crashes to the ground. While a juggler can relax once he gets into a rhythm, there is no rest for the spinner. To keep the plates spinning, he has to keep running. To me, that's what being a working parent feels like. Spinning plates.

Is this a good way to live? No. In an ideal world, we'd all spend a lot of time reclining in a hammock, twiddling our thumbs and wondering what to do next. We'd get eight hours sleep a night, play with our kids, then stroll off to our part-time job at the end of the street, chatting with our neighbours along the way.

But that's not the reality. At certain critical stages – usually in our peak productive years of our 30s and 40s – life is so busy it can become a serious health hazard. Some analysts believe we're addicted to being busy: that being busy is a status symbol and we use our level of 'busyness' as a sign of how important we are.

For some people – compulsively busy workaholics, for example – this may indeed be the case. But for most of us, the extreme busyness of our lives is not a conscious choice – it's just the unavoidable by-product of working and having kids and trying to do all the things we're meant to do as responsible citizens.

'Everyone talks as if you are stupid if you don't meditate, do yoga, walk for 20 minutes and read all instructions carefully before use. You're also meant to check the batteries in your fire alarm, supervise your children's homework, make soup from scratch and adjust your wing mirrors before ever putting the car in gear,' columnist Richard Glover wrote in *The Sydney Morning Herald*.

'If we did everything demanded of us by public health officials, mental health experts and safety campaigners, we'd need 300 hours in every day, would never be able to sleep or work and would still wake up every morning with this vague feeling of guilt and underachievement.'[5]

There's no doubt that lack of time is one of the major stress factors of modern life. But there's also a lot to love about this crazy age we live in. Never before have we had the opportunity to experience so much of what the world has to offer. Our potential for a long and adventurous life far outstrips anything our parents could have imagined thanks to advances in medicine and technology, more progressive attitudes and a higher standard of living.

If we want a successful career, a comfortable home, kids and a circle of friends – hey, it's all possible. Whether we've still got time to eat properly – well, that's another matter altogether.

Like cooking, lack of time was never really a problem for me before I got married and had kids. Naturally I whinged about how busy I was, but I was busy doing things like getting manicures, going to the gym and touring Europe.

I didn't know what busy was until I had kids. Then it hit me like a ton of bricks. Being really, truly busy was very different indeed. A busy day was no longer one where I had to choose between getting my hair done and having lunch with a friend. A busy day was one where I had to choose between showering and eating. Or making the kids' dinner and getting to work on time.

In that way, the old pressure cooker really did save my life. Once I got into the swing of bulk cooking and freezing at super-fast speeds, I calculated that it saved me around 45 minutes a day. That might not sound a lot to somebody who has plenty of time on their hands, but when you don't, 45 extra minutes a day is like 45 ounces of pure gold.

Using the pressure cooker made an immediate, quantifiable change to my life. And with that extra 45 minutes a day, I started thinking about other ways to save time. I'm no physics expert, but I do get the concept that time is a fairly fluid concept. An hour can often seem like a minute, and vice versa. Maybe, I thought, there was a way to stretch time, and squeeze it, so that all the wonderful things in life – family, friends, career, leisure – could fit seamlessly into it without crowding each other and fighting for space.

There's only 24 hours in a day, people say. Actually, there's more. You just have to know where they're hiding.

Time Squeezing

I stumbled across this delicious phrase in a research paper called, 'How do they do it? ... How working mothers find time for the kids'.[6] The study was prompted by one of the paradoxes of modern life: as women spend more and more hours in the workforce, they have also increased the amount of time they spend with their children. The big mystery is, with only 24 hours in a day, where are they getting that extra kid-time from?

For me, the idea of 'squeezing time' to get more hours out of the day was a perfect analogy. It's a bit like an orange. No matter how much you squeeze it, there always seems to be one more drop that you can get out of it.

Time squeezing is similar to multi-tasking, but it takes the concept one step further. Squeezing those extra few minutes out of every hour requires actively looking for opportunities to do more than one thing at once. The best time to squeeze is the time you spend doing fairly mindless tasks, like waiting on hold, or watching television. Multi-tasking at those times will leave you free to give your undivided attention to the things that really count, like playing with your kids or having a soak in the bath.

While I'm generally not a fan of technology and how it rules our lives, it can be a huge help when doing two things at once. Here are a few simple examples.

- Invest in a bluetooth hands-free device and make your phone calls while grocery shopping/watching the kids at the park.
- Get a home phone with a loudspeaker so you can do other things while waiting on hold to call centres (I've been able to cook an entire meal while waiting to get through to Telstra).
- Listen to relaxation CDs or audio books for a bit of 'me time' if you have a long commute.

Once you start looking for opportunities to squeeze time you'll be amazed at how many there are. While many of them only yield a few extra minutes, occasionally you'll stumble across a goldmine.

This book is, in fact, a triumph of time squeezing. When I was first commissioned to write it, I had serious doubts about whether I'd have the time to do it. But when I analysed my day, I realised I had two whole hours of underutilised time: the long drive to and from work. So I bought a small tape recorder and spent the whole two hours talking into it. Later, I'd transcribe the tape and write it up whenever a 15-minute block of time became available. Now, when people ask me how I had the time to write a 50 000-word book on having no time, I can honestly say: I did most of it on the way to work.

Time squeezing and pressure cooking

The pressure cooker is an ideal time-squeeze machine. Once you've put all your ingredients inside and closed the lid there's nothing more to do until it's finished. No stirring, no checking, no adjusting temperature. You can then squeeze more out of that 15 to 20 minutes of cooking time by doing something else. Emptying the garbage bin, putting on a load of washing, calling your personal stylist – you know the kind of stuff.

Time Shifting

The term 'time shifting' originated in the 1970s with the advent of the VCR. The new video recording machines allowed people to tape their favourite programs and 'shift' their viewing to a more convenient time. But more recently, it's been adopted as a metaphor by the booming time-management industry as a way of fitting more tasks into your day.

I don't have time to read time-management books, so I don't know how the experts would define time shifting. But when I first heard the phrase, it seemed self-evident. Time shifting is something that busy people do instinctively. When I asked the ABC's medical reporter Sophie Scott – author, full-time journalist and mother of two – for her top time-saving technique, she said immediately: 'Doing the laundry at 10 o'clock at night when everyone's in bed.' A classic time shift!

At its most basic, time shifting simply means deferring a task to a more convenient time. For many of us, this is a no-brainer – organised people do it without thinking. But it doesn't come so easily to everyone. If you know someone whose life is disorganised and chaotic, you'll notice that their attempts to time shift usually only go halfway. They get the first bit right – deferring the task – but it's the second bit – actually doing it – where they fall apart. By delaying, they buy themselves some time in the short-term, but inevitably, the undone task comes back to haunt them, usually at the most inconvenient time. By then it's become so critical that shifting it to later is no longer an option, it has to be done 'NOW!' – and other things suffer as a consequence. Maximum stress.

Unlike procrastination, time shifting does not mean putting something off, or not doing it at all. It means assigning it a place on your list of priorities and doing it at the first available opportunity.

To me, time shifting also means delegating. Instead of moving a task to a more convenient time, you move it to a more convenient person. As a result, the time you would have invested in that particular task has now been 'shifted' onto someone else's schedule. A personal assistant would be ideal. But if you don't have one, any warm, breathing body will do. My children, for example, have been pressed into service from the age of two when they were first able to fetch and carry without too many accidents. I figure at their age their schedule can handle it – muscle in on it!

Time shifting and pressure cooking

Regular cooking is less flexible than pressure cooking because it takes a lot longer and it's harder to shift in a packed schedule. Not many of us have one-hour windows of free time in the day to which we can relocate it. Most pressure cooking recipes, on the other hand, only take 10 to 15 minutes. That's a much easier block of time to relocate – even busy people frequently have short bursts of free time in-between tasks. This is one of the main reasons pressure cooking is ideal for very busy people – you can fit it in to a very short window of time, when one unexpectedly becomes available.

Time Blocking

The peak of my work/family stress load came when I returned to work after the birth of my second child. Suddenly I was juggling a baby, a toddler, a job, a marriage, a house and a two-hour daily commute. On paper, the logistics were impossible. If I tallied up the hours required to do everything properly it worked out to more than 24 (and that was without sleeping). But as every working parent discovers, when you don't have a choice, you figure out a way.

Finding a solution became my obsession. I lay awake between the night feeds racking my addled brain for a way to make things easier. Throughout each frantic day, as one task piled upon another with no respite, I kept mental notes and reviewed them during the long drive to and from work. The problem was not so much the number of tasks, I realised, as the haphazard way in which I was doing them. I needed to prioritise.

At first, I started categorising tasks as either 'big' or 'small'. I calculated that on a reasonably normal day, I could accomplish one 'big' task (such as taking the children to the doctor), as well as 5 to 6 'small' tasks, like putting on a load of washing or picking up some groceries before going to work. My first basic attempt at time management was to limit myself to a set number of 'big' and 'small' tasks. On some days, I might have two big tasks to do, and all the small ones would have to fall by the wayside. On other days, I might have a run of a dozen small errands to carry out, but nothing too big or time-consuming.

As time went on I realised that most small tasks took an average of 15 minutes. It took 15 minutes to do the washing up, 15 minutes to fold a full basket of laundry, 15 minutes to put it all away. It took me 15 minutes to drive to the supermarket, 15 minutes to whizz up and down the aisles, and 15 minutes to get through the checkout. Making soup in the pressure cooker took 10 minutes to prepare the ingredients, and five minutes of cooking time. Bigger tasks took multiples of 15 minutes.

Dividing the day into 15-minute blocks of time, with each task allotted either single or multiple blocks, somehow made it seem more manageable. Having a 15-minute deadline for each dreary domestic job forced me not to dawdle and procrastinate. If I finished a task early, I'd use the spare five minutes to make a quick phone call. If I stuck to my timetable, I'd reward myself by stopping at the local cafe on my way to work to have a coffee and read the papers – as long as I was out within 15 minutes. If friends called from overseas, instead of chatting for an hour or more, I'd explain I only had 15 minutes. If somebody asked me for a favour that was going to take more than 15 minutes of my time, I said no. (The other benefit of saying 'no' to people who ask for favours is that they eventually stop asking!)

Does this sound mad? Looking back, it certainly seems that way. But I know, with absolute certainty, that it was the only way I managed to cope. Dividing the day into 15-minute blocks also made me appreciate how much time I had previously wasted on things like email. Under the 15-minute rule, I checked my email at home just once a day, quickly sent off brief replies, and moved on to the next task.

Limiting each task to 15 minutes quickly paid dividends. Almost immediately, I started accomplishing more and feeling less stressed. As rigid as the system was, it also had an unexpected benefit: it revealed occasional, precious blocks of free time. Whereas before I would have squandered a free 15-minutes without even noticing, the new system forced me to appreciate that time for what it was: a block of pure gold.

Hidden Time

If you're feeling pressured by a chronic lack of time, it's worth analysing your day to find out where those golden nuggets are hiding. You can then 'block' that time and put it to better use.

So where had that extra time been hiding? Like most busy people, I always thought I was highly efficient with my time. But it only took a bit of amateur sleuthing to realise I was actually wasting a fair bit of it. The free time was there, but it was being taken up by a range of fairly useless activities that were little more than habits.

If you're feeling pressured by a chronic lack of time, it's worth analysing your day to find out where those golden nuggets are hiding. You can then 'block' that time and put it to better use. Here are a few places worth looking.

Television

As much as I hate to bite the hand that feeds me, this is the greatest time waster of our age. A certain amount of it can be relaxing, but it's all too easy to start watching and still be there, glassy-eyed, five hours later. I still watch TV, but only if I'm doing something else at the same time, like ironing or paying bills on the internet (time squeezing). When you're exhausted after a day of work and childcare, it's tempting to slump in front of the telly as some kind of reward. But limiting your viewing, or stopping it altogether, will increase the time you have for more important things, including sleep. (In the interests of full disclosure, I admit that my one vice is watching *The Bold and the Beautiful* every afternoon while I'm getting made up for the news. It's only because I'm stuck in the chair and can't do anything else. That's my excuse and I'm sticking to it.)

Recreational shopping

Women in particular have a weakness for shopping for shopping's sake. It's a huge waste of time and money. There is only one solution: stay away from the shops! Buying stuff for the temporary high it produces is an addiction, and the best way to break it is going cold turkey. Often this happens automatically as life becomes busier.

I remember feeling puzzled when, after six months of no shopping, I finally had a child-free afternoon to spend at the shopping mall. To my amazement, I couldn't find anything I was interested in buying. Not one thing. And as long as I stay away from shopping centres, my lack of interest persists. If I stray into one and purchase a single item, the addiction kicks in again, and before I know it I'm loading half a dozen bags into the car.

With recreational shopping, as with so many other useless pursuits, it all boils down to three little words: Just Say No.

Technology

Gadgets were meant to be our friends. They were meant to help us and save us time. Now they've taken over our lives and they rule the planet.

But a growing number of people are rebelling against the tyranny of mobile phones, iPods and the like. As most of us eventually realise, rather than connecting people, they can be isolating and anti-social.

But there's another good reason to wean ourselves off gadgets: they take up an awful lot of time. For every new gadget (a laptop with mobile broadband, let's say) you have to spend hours researching the options. Then you spend an hour or two at the shop waiting to be served and signing a contract. Then you spend an hour poring over the instruction booklet before discovering it doesn't work. More hours back at the shop ('It's not our problem, we're just a retail outlet') and on the phone to the hilariously named Help Desk. You find the time to drop it off to be fixed, and then to pick it up again. Then once you've got it working, you've only got about 12 months before it's totally out of date and needs to be replaced.

Mobile phones with cameras in them are another good example. You spend all that time taking photos on your phone and then what happens to them? Does anybody actually have the time to download the photos and print them out? Or do they all just disappear when you upgrade your phone to one that has an even better camera?

Personally, I dropped out of the technology race when iPods came along because I didn't have the time to figure out how to download songs. I just gave up. It's like age rings on a tree – you can tell how old somebody is by the technology that finally defeats them.

Internet and email

As essential as the internet is, it runs a very close second to television as one of life's great time wasters.

The two biggest culprits are email and social networking sites like Facebook. As an exercise, keep a note of how many times a day you check your emails. More than a dozen would not be unusual (recent studies show the average employee checks their email 42 times a day). [7] Some people are permanently connected to their inbox via mobile phones and PDAs.

Facebooking is a whole other type of quicksand. Before you know it, you're being hounded by everyone you ever knew, or never knew. The modern compulsion to be connected 24/7 is not only stressful, it's time-consuming. Being aware of just how much time you spend online is the first step to cutting it back.

Being Organised

To some people, being organised comes naturally. For others, it's a hard slog. But whatever category you fall into, there's no escaping it: a busy life needs to be an organised life, or it (and you) will collapse. As uber-housewife Martha Stewart says, life is too complicated not to be orderly. People juggling work and young families in particular find the sheer number of competing demands overwhelming. Instilling some sense of order and predictability into an otherwise chaotic environment is the only way you'll get through those challenging years with your physical and mental health intact.

The only drawback to getting yourself organised is that it does initially take time. But once you've got systems in place, things start ticking over automatically. You'll still need to check your systems periodically and adjust them when necessary. But spending a few minutes each day doing that will save you years of stress and frustration in the long run.

When it comes to organising your life, you need to invest time to save time. Here are some of the essentials I can't do without.

A filing cabinet

I'm not talking about one of those flimsy cardboard concertina things you stick your tax receipts in. I'm talking about a serious filing cabinet, a big heavy metal thing that weighs a ton, with lots of hanging files in it. If you can move it on your own, it's not going to do the job.

Before I had kids, I shared a house with a single mother who was fiendishly well organised. Her key tool was a large metal filing cabinet which contained virtually every document relevant to her and her son's life. At the time, I was puzzled by the importance she placed on it. I mean, how much paperwork could one small child generate?

A few years later, when I had two of them myself, I realised the birth certificate was just the start of it.

Having a family involves an endless and overwhelming deluge of paperwork which arrives daily. Much of it can be thrown away, but there's an awful lot that needs to be accessed on either a regular or occasional basis. There's car insurance, house insurance, health insurance, mortgage documents, bank statements and pay slips. The kids' health records and immunisation certificates. The last seven years' tax returns. Warranties for the 250 different gadgets and appliances in your home. Contracts with gyms and mobile phone companies that lock you up until you die. And when you do ... where's the will? Not that you'd care by then, but someone else will when they find it under 'W' in the filing cabinet – and they'll thank you for it.

THE THRIFTY PARENT re-gifts unused baby clothes. New parents are usually inundated with masses of gorgeous designer clothes for newborns that they never get around to using before their baby grows out of them. Keep the tags attached and pass them on. Also, ask friends and family to give clothes in bigger sizes, rather than 0000, so your baby will actually get to wear them.

The key to a successful filing system is not just putting things into it, but being able to find them again. So the first step is to spend an hour or so labelling your files in a way that makes sense to you. The next step is to actually put stuff in there (on a daily basis if possible) so it doesn't get on top of you. When I open the mail at the end of the day I either file things immediately, put them in the 'to do' folder, or chuck them.

It's just as important to clean out the filing cabinet. Every six months I take a 15-minute block of time to go through the files and throw away anything that's no longer needed. If you don't regularly flush out the filing system – in with the new, out with the old – it becomes so overstuffed you can't find anything.

Some important documents – like instruction booklets and X-rays – are difficult to file because of their size. For that reason, I use a 3-door cabinet. The top two drawers are for hanging files and the bottom drawer is for oversize documents, with a separate box for receipts, instruction manuals and warranties.

If you are short on space, consider a lateral filing cabinet. These are wider and more shallow than the traditional cabinets, which are tall and bulky and stick out a long way. The lateral filing system allows you to hang the files north–south as well as east–west. They take up less space and they look better.

If it all sounds too hard, just remember: managing a family is like running a business. And just like a business owner, you need a good office and filing system to keep it all under control.

Tip

THE THRIFTY HOUSEKEEPER can pick up all kinds of filing cabinets, including the more stylish lateral ones, on eBay for about a tenth of the full retail price.

Decluttering

The more stuff you have, the more time you have to spend tidying it, storing it, then finding it when you need it. Creating clear space in your home also makes it a more tranquil and pleasant place to be. Once children arrive, stuff accumulates at an alarming rate, and before you know it, you'll have to climb over a mountain of old prams, toys and high chairs just to get out the door.

The only solution is to regularly purge. Once a month, if you can manage it, spend an hour collecting obsolete stuff and taking it to the local charity shop. Resist the urge to hang onto old baby clothes for sentimental reasons. Pass them on to someone else as soon as your kids outgrow them. One family I know held a garage sale every six months during the mortgage crisis – it covered their interest rate rises and also kept the house clear of clutter.

An old fashioned diary
Before PDAs, there was the Filofax. Everybody had one, and to my mind, an old-style diary still beats the new technology hands down. The good old pen-and-paper system is simply more efficient time-wise, and easier to use. Visually, it's easier to get a grip on the week ahead when it's all there in front of you in black and white. Diaries also have various pockets for stowing business cards, bills and other bits and pieces that come in handy.

'An old fashioned diary is best for visual people like me. Electronic organisers and computers are great for sorting, but the screen isn't open all day. A diary is the best technique for jogging your memory and keeping to your priority list,' says Dr Judith Slocombe, mother of nine and CEO of the Alannah and Madeline Foundation. [8]

Pin and password book
As well as a diary, which I take everywhere, I have a separate, smaller book at home, where I note down all my logins, passwords and PINs for various accounts and websites. There are scores of them! It's the only way I can keep track. But for security reasons, I never take my PIN and password book outside the house.

Internet or automatic payments
This is one area in which new technology has been incredibly helpful. Paying your bills over the internet can save enormous time and stress, however there are some things to be wary of.

Organising your bills to be paid automatically has many benefits, including peace of mind – you no longer have to worry about whether the phone's going to be cut off because you've forgotten to pay the bill. On the downside, having your bills out of sight and out of mind means you can overlook mistakes and overcharging (I found this to be a particular problem with a big telecoms company). And if you have payments automatically put on your credit card (as opposed to being debited from a savings account), it can be extraordinarily difficult to cancel them. For those reasons, I pay most of my bills through BPAY, as they come in, so I can check the statement. I've set up automatic payments (from a savings account) for long-term services such as car tolls, water and electricity, where the amounts are relatively small and any discrepancies are easy to spot. I never make any automatic payments on credit card due to the complicated process required to cancel them.

Culling technology and household appliances

The more gadgets you have, the more time it takes to learn how to use them and get them fixed when they break. The fewer you have, the simpler life is. A lot of technology is helpful, even essential, in today's world. But before you invest time and money in the very latest thing, ask yourself if you really need it.

Mobile phones are a good example. For most of us, they're indispensable. In fact, they're so cheap and convenient that a lot of people don't even bother with a landline any more. But unless you really need to receive emails and take photos with one, then stick to a very basic pre-paid phone as opposed to a fancy one on a long contract. That way, if it breaks or you lose it, there's no hassle, you just buy another one.

However many gadgets and appliances you end up with (and it

could be hundreds, including the electronic thermometer you stick in your baby's ear), make sure you have a system for keeping all the receipts, instruction manuals and warranties in one place because they *will* break down and you *will* forget how to use them. I have two large A4-sized boxes that, despite regular culling, are permanently bursting with gadget paperwork.

Keep It Simple

The key to creating more time in your life is to simplify it. Less stuff = more time. Here are some practical suggestions that have worked for me, or people I know. Everybody's circumstances are different, and they change depending on whether you work, your type of work, whether you have kids, and how old they are. But all are worth considering.

- Disconnect your landline telephone and use only pre-paid, basic mobile phones.
- Ruthlessly purge your kitchen gadgets. Unless you use something at least once a week, get rid of it.
- The only household appliance that is truly time-saving (apart from a pressure cooker) is a washing machine. We've been brainwashed into thinking that every home needs a microwave, a dishwasher, a tumble drier and a telephone with a digital answering machine. It's only recently that I've got rid of all these things and not noticed any difference.
- Strip your working wardrobe back to the basics. 'A while ago I decided to "uniform" myself for work because I wasted so much time staring into my wardrobe trying to decide what to wear,' says ABC stylist Chris Sall. 'I bought five black shirts and some black pants, and now the whole week is sorted. Black is my work uniform. It always looks good, and it's one less decision to make.'

- Invest in bluetooth technology and make your essential phone calls during commuting or shopping time.
- Switch off your voicemail service. If it's important, they'll get back to you. 'I've switched off voicemail and it's changed my life. I got rid of it and it's reduced my stress levels. It trains colleagues that I'm not the go-to person. My staff manage my phone during the day,' says Tory Archibald, single mother and MD of Torstar Communications, a marketing company.[9]
- Check your emails once a day. If necessary, organise an automatic reply to emails that lets people know you are not constantly checking them. If you work part-time, make sure you only check your emails on the days you work, and send an automatic reply so everybody is aware what those days are. It helps to train people (including staff, clients, friends and family) that you are not available 24/7.
- Set yourself a two-minute limit on replying to work-related emails. Keep it short and sharp and, if possible, reply as soon as you receive it. Then you can forget it.
- Remove yourself from Facebook (or whatever social-networking site you waste your time on) or at least put it on hold until life becomes more manageable. Do you really want to spend a sizeable chunk of your day processing 'friend requests' from people you knew 25 years ago and have no interest in?
- Learn to say, 'can I check my diary and get back to you?' when people invite you to a social event or ask you for a favour. All too often, we automatically say yes, only to find ourselves overwhelmed. Think about it for a day or two before committing your time to something.
- Cull your friends. More accurately, cull your acquaintances. Most of us are lucky to have a handful of real friends in our lifetime. Focus

on them, not the multitudes who provide temporary amusement but ultimately don't count. It sounds brutal, but you know it's true.

• Just say *no* to as many inconsequential requests as you possibly can. When the local barista asks you if you'd like a loyalty card, just say no (like you need more stuff in your wallet, right?). When the shop assistant at a boutique wants to put you on the mailing list as a VIP customer, just say no (otherwise you'll be inundated with text messages and brochures in the mail). If you've still got a landline telephone, make sure you have an unlisted number so you don't have to deal with dozens of marketing calls. Tick the box: no, no, no! It's a great word. It's empowering and liberating. Use it often.

Of course, there are several things in life that cannot be time-managed out of existence. We need to work a certain number of hours, or we don't get paid. We want to spend time with our children, for our sake and theirs. And, like it or not, we have to spend a big chunk of our time doing that thing that everybody hates. Housework.

'Going to the beach was so simple when we were kids. We'd all jump in the car – six kids plus mum and dad – wind down the windows to get some air, and drive down to the Gold Coast. No seatbelts, being the 1970s. We'd play on the beach all day, get sunburnt, and on the way home to Brisbane, we'd buy hot chips. That was it: beach, play, sunburn, chips. If we were lucky we'd get an ice-cream. These days, you can't leave the house until the kids are covered in sunscreen and neck-to-knee sunsuits and a hat. You sit in a traffic jam for two hours, and fight with a million other people for a parking spot. The kids aren't allowed to eat ice-cream or hot chips because of fat and allergies, and you have to keep them out of the sun between 10 am and 2 pm. It's the beach, for crying out loud!

What happened?'

Debbie, 46

I hate
housework!
you make
the beds, you
wash the
dishes, and
six months
later you have
to start all
over again!

Joan Rivers

home

In the space of one or two generations we've experienced the most
phenomenal social and technological changes in our history. My
grandmother used to cook damper over hot coals in a hole in the
ground; I can zap mass-produced frozen meals in a microwave.
And that's within living memory. Incredible.

home

MY FAVOURITE JOKE ABOUT HOUSEWORK goes along these lines. A man arrives home from a hard day at work to find the house in chaos. The sink's full of dirty dishes, there's damp laundry sitting in the washing machine, the baby's running around crying with a full nappy and the toddler is tossing CDs off the back deck. His wife is nowhere in sight. Frantically, fearing something disastrous has happened, he searches the house, and eventually finds her sitting up in bed in her nightie, calmly eating chocolates and watching *The Bold and the Beautiful.*

'What happened?' he gasps.

The wife turns down the volume with the remote and says, 'You know how you always ask me what I do all day? Well, today I didn't do it.'

Here's the thing about housework, though: it's no joke. It's serious stuff. Unpaid domestic labour – including caring for children – keeps the economy rolling by supporting the taxpayers who fund it, and raising the future taxpayers who'll take over from them. 'All of the developed economies of the world depend on the unpaid work of housewives,' according to Ruth Cowan, an American scholar who's spent several decades studying (and doing) housework. [10]

But because housework doesn't directly put any cash into the system, it's been largely ignored by politicians and economists. Unpaid household work, including childcare, is not officially considered part of Australia's economic output. However, when it is taken into account, it represents nearly half of GDP [11] – without it, our economy would collapse.

Historians, too, haven't been very interested in domestic labour, for, well, all of history. It was only in 2006 that the Australian census included questions about 'unpaid work', to figure out how much of it was being done, who was doing it, and how much time it took up.

So while housework is largely unrecognised, it's incredibly important, both economically and socially. It is also the most common cause of arguments within Australian households: the row over who does what.

When it comes to solving the issue of work/life balance, the mundane realities of housework and childcare cannot be ignored. Far from being, as social commentator Bettina Arndt claims, 'only a tiny part of the real deal', it's the root of the entire problem. [12]

Hey Guys, Want More Sex?

Sure you do! Now I've got your attention, here are four good reasons, according to scientists, men should do more housework.

1   It's true – your wives really will have sex with you more often. Studies show the more housework a man does, the more attractive his wife finds him. 'Therapists say there's a direct correlation between men doing more housework and the frequency of sex, and wives reported greater feelings of sexual interest ... for husbands who participated in housework,' a report for the US Council

on Contemporary Families found.[13] And in 2007, University of Kentucky researchers found that the happier a wife was with her husband's contribution to domestic chores, the more often they had sex – and the less likely she was to have an affair.[14] Australian researchers stumbled on the issue unexpectedly while interviewing working mothers, some of whom said that they had withheld sex from their lazy husbands as punishment.[15] So exactly how much housework do you need to do to get more sex? Well boys … you'll just have to try it and see. (Of course, after doing the housework you'll be too tired for sex. That's kind of the way it goes.)

2   Men who clean are more likely to become a dad. A recent British study found that working women were much more likely to have a baby if their husbands did a reasonable share of the housework. [16] This is backed up by Australian research, which found that domestic 'fairness' has a bearing on whether couples go on to have a second child. [17] It might also explain why Italy – where men do virtually none of the domestic work – has one of the lowest birth rates in the developed world, and why helpful Norwegian men are making more babies than anyone else in the developed world. [18]

3   Men who do housework are less likely to get divorced. [19] Studies here and overseas have found a direct link between how much housework a husband does and the longevity of a marriage.

4   Men who do housework live longer. A study by the University of Victoria in Canada found that although men had more leisure time than women, they did not spend it engaged in 'meaningful activity' and might literally die of boredom. While women busied themselves with housework and life goals, blokes spent a lot of their free time watching TV, playing computer games or doing nothing. [20] What's so bad about that, you may ask? Well, apparently they also get bored and lonely as a result, and there's a strong link between emotions

and mortality. 'There's an argument it might be worthwhile [for] men to exchange some of their leisure time for a higher participation in unpaid work,' said Dr Leonie Bloomfield, the psychologist in charge of the study. 'Some of [their] time could be spent engaged in domestic work or increasing their participation in childcare.' [21]

The Great Domestic Divide

If we're going to crack the whole work/family dilemma, we have to get our heads around the housework issue. The unequal division of domestic labour, and the inflexible work practices that entrench it, are two of the biggest issues facing Australian families.

Studies consistently find that work/family strain remains a particular problem for women. 'It is women who are disproportionately subject to work/family strain, because responsibility for childcare and housework in Australia is still predominantly women's work', according to a report by the Social Policy Research Centre. [22] 'Fathers are more likely to have someone to take over, to be able to avoid the less pleasant and more urgent tasks, and rarely do other tasks such as childcare.' [23]

As more and more women have joined the workforce, their domestic responsibilities have barely changed. Australian statistics show that a stay-at-home mum does around 77 hours of unpaid work per week (caring for a newborn baby alone can take up to 90 hours). If she takes a part-time job to help with the mortgage, she'll still be doing 69 hours of domestic work on top of that. A mother who works full-time does less housework and childcare – around 57 hours on top of her 40-hour week in the workforce. Even a woman who works very long hours (more than 49 hours a week) still does 54 hours of domestic work on top of that.[24]

Men's contribution, on the other hand, does not vary, regardless of whether their wife works. They do a flat rate of 30 hours a week. But studies show it is usually a different kind of domestic work – non-urgent tasks, done at their discretion, such as lawn-mowing and playing with the kids. Women are the ones who do the daily drudge work of cooking, cleaning, laundry and supervising children, often juggling several tasks at once.[25]

The gap between men and women is narrowing, but at a glacial pace. Studies consistently find that women do at least twice as much domestic work as men, sometimes three or four times as much, regardless of whether they also have a paying job.

Getting married immediately and dramatically increases the amount of housework a woman does; for men, getting married reduces their housework.[26] And when children come along, the Great Divide becomes even wider.

The parent trap
Part of the problem is the stubborn refusal of Australia's employers to change their old-fashioned attitudes so that men have the time to step up and meet their family responsibilities. While many businesses pay lip-service to family-friendly policies, in practice they still operate on the old model of a full-time male breadwinner, with a wife at home looking after the house and the kids. In their heads, that's still the way it works.

Any worker who bucks this outdated view of the world – and it's usually a woman with children – is considered a nuisance. No-one would ever say it publicly, of course. But that's my opinion, based on 30 years in an industry which, ironically, is dominated by women.

'They're a rostering nightmare, all these part-time mums,' one manager said to me quite openly. 'They all want this day or that day to fit in with childcare. They don't seem to appreciate what a headache it is.'

104

When I worked overseas, a highly regarded producer announced she was pregnant. She was told to be back at work full-time within three months of giving birth – or leave. 'Don't expect special treatment just because you're having a baby,' the boss told her bluntly. 'If you don't want to work the overnight shift, then quit and go casual.' She quit and left the industry.

The anecdotal evidence is backed up by research, which shows that women continue to be fired or demoted simply because they have children. Despite 30 years of supposed protection under the *Sex Discrimination Act*, a recent report found that a 'culture of antagonism' exists towards female workers who are pregnant or on maternity leave. The Pregnant Pause study was based on the experiences of 76 women who requested legal help over a five-month period from the Women's Employment Rights Project in Sydney. Half of them had lost their jobs. [27]

No wonder men aren't queuing up to demand more flexible working conditions. They've seen what's happened to their wives.

'Marginalisation, job insecurity, missing out on promotions – these are all features of the dreaded "daddy track" that young fathers fear they'll be put onto if they take too much time off work to care for their children,' says Elizabeth Broderick, the Federal Sex Discrimination Commissioner. [28]

Wedlock deadlock

But bosses aren't the only ones hanging on to quaint attitudes. 'We have the same argument about every 10 days,' says my friend Kate, a part-time working mum. 'Steve's attitude is that because he's the main breadwinner, his time at home is time for him to relax. If I ask him to do something domestic, he says, "You're at home all day, Kate – you do it." As if "being home all day" with three children means I sit around relaxing! I have to remind him constantly that I also work three days a week. But for some reason that doesn't seem to count.'

makes

a

Happ

Hom

The war over [domestic] fairness is corrosive. It eats the heart out of loving relationships. She burns with resentment. He feels deeply misunderstood. Couples who have lived together, gone to birthing classes together, find their relationship, 10 years and two children later, fraying at the edge over the fairness issue. [29] Adele Horin, *The Sydney Morning Herald*

How much is a wife worth?

Not only does the unfair division of domestic work cause tension between spouses, it places enormous time pressure on women. Those who stay at home with young children are effectively doing two full-time jobs simultaneously, especially when they have more than one child under five. (And if you don't believe that childcare and housework are two separate jobs, try asking a cleaner to look after the kids, or asking a nanny to do the cooking, cleaning, shopping, laundry, preschool duties and banking.)

According to the salary.com website, the value of a full-time homemaker with three children, in Australian currency, is around $140 000 per year (or the equivalent of $US117 000, according to their 'mom salary' calculator).

As for women who also work outside the home, they effectively have three shifts to do – paid work, housework and childcare. Most women with young children are on duty seven days a week, and at all times of the night and day. Holidays are often a case of 'same stuff, different location', with many women still responsible for organising, cooking and cleaning while the rest of the family relaxes. (This is one of the reasons why the traditional Australian summer holiday at the beach is fast disappearing in favour of overseas resorts where someone else cooks the meals and makes the beds.)

So for mothers with young children – and especially those who also work outside the home – there are usually no weekends, no real holidays, no sick leave, and they're on call 24/7. No wonder mothers with children under five are officially the most time-poor members of our society. [30]

Balancing the scales

Things aren't easy for men today, either. The days of a job for life, a 38-hour week and a gold watch on retirement are long gone. Men are working longer hours, with less security, in industries that increasingly rely on short-term contracts. A Sydney University study of 8 000 workers found that 30 per cent are in precarious employment, including part-time or casual work. More than half of all workers are struggling to get by financially and say that more and more is expected of them for the same pay. Forty per cent of men work more than 50 hours a week, well above the OECD average. [31]

Those on high salaries, meanwhile, are expected to work even harder, doing 60-to-80 hour weeks to safeguard their positions in a cut-throat corporate world that barely recognises that workers have families. It's hard enough for a woman to slink out of the office at 5.30 pm to pick up the kids from childcare; for a high-earning man, it's career suicide.

And once they get home after working the longest hours in the developed world, today's men are also expected to share the housework and look after their children. There's no doubt that in some households, men already do their fair share of the domestic duties. The absentee, workaholic husband is a dying breed: three quarters of men say they would be happy to take a pay-cut to work fewer hours.

As well, there's been a seismic shift in fatherhood, with most men keen to play a much bigger role in the lives of their children. It's interesting that as they do, they're also becoming more prone to something once considered the sole preserve of women: post-natal depression. While this area of research is still in its infancy, it's estimated that up to 10 per cent of first-time fathers experience post-natal depression, compared to up to 15 per cent of first-time mothers. [32]

Still, there are plenty of other areas where traditional breadwinners have a lot of catching up to do. Currently, Australian men spend only a minute a day engaged in the sole care of their children, Monday to Friday – and most of those 60 seconds is spent doing fun stuff like playing and reading. The drudge work of childcare, such as bathing and feeding, is left to their wives.[33]

And those wives are increasingly fed up with the deal. Unlike the 'superwomen' of the 1970s and '80s, they are no longer willing to do it all in exchange for the privilege of having a career. They're getting snappy about it, and that's causing conflict.

Here's a classic example: Lou and Craig have two young children. Lou works three days a week outside the home and Craig works six or seven long days a week running his small business. Lou was telling me how they'd had a huge row at 2 am the previous night. The issue: whose turn was it to get up to a crying baby?

'I've already been up to her twice, it's your turn,' Lou said.

'I shouldn't have to get up in the middle of the night,' Craig replied. 'I work 80 hours a week.'

'So do I,' said Lou. 'I get up when you get up, and I go to bed when you go to bed. In between, just like you, I'm working. The only difference is I don't get paid for most of it, and nobody tells me how clever I am.'

'I'm exhausted,' said Craig.

'So am I,' said Lou. 'I've been looking after the kids all day and I haven't got to sleep yet. I may as well be a single mother.'

'Well … if I have to get up to the baby all the time, I won't be able to do my job properly,' said Craig.

'Same here,' said Lou. 'My job is looking after the kids, the house, and you, as well as going to work. At some point, I have to sleep.' Craig gave in and got up. Lou lay there feeling guilty.

Sound familiar? Variations of that argument happen every night around Australia. If the story proves anything, it's just how hard it's become to draw the line when dividing domestic duties. Who's to say what's fair and what's not? Who's to say whose work is more 'important', and should that make any difference when it comes to doing the dirty work? Every couple's situation is different. There's no template. We just have to figure it out for ourselves.

A Bit of History

The division of domestic labour has become a hot topic in recent years because of the large numbers of women in the workforce. We tend to think of that as a fairly recent trend. In fact, Australia has a long, proud history of frazzled housewives trying to squeeze their paying jobs in between the domestic chores.

Ethel Turner, one of Australia's most beloved authors, was dealing with exactly the same issues more than a hundred years ago. At a time when middle-class women rarely worked outside the home, Ethel had a successful, high-powered career as a writer, which went stratospheric after *Seven Little Australians* was published. She also had two young children and a house to manage, and her diaries are full of the daily annoyances and tedium of domestic chores, which constantly interrupted her work.

'Mornings very busy with housework,' she wrote in 1897. 'Despite the trouble servants are, I wouldn't be without [one] permanently – it is such a shocking waste of time doing all the thousand and one details of work in a house. Nellie to start tomorrow.' [34]

Nellie was just the latest in an endless succession of servants, most of them unsuitable, unwilling or just plain useless. Ethel was constantly 'vexed' by the problem of finding reliable domestic help. Some of the girls lasted only a few days. Once Ethel had children, and with her career in full flight, her need for domestic support became even more urgent.

'I don't think 48 hours to the day would see all my work finished … and then there is shopping. And the calls of one's family – and the rights of a husband to have me at leisure in the evening, and letters, and accounts, and, and, and …' she wrote in 1902, with a desperation many modern women could relate to.

Luckily, her husband Herbert Curlewis, a barrister, was also ahead of his time. On busy days he used to pack Ethel off to bed to rest while he did the washing up. (That was pretty good for those days. Now, of course, a helpful husband would also change the garbage bin liner, clean the inside of the microwave, notice that the vacuum cleaner needs a new bag, and de-fluff the lint filter in the tumble drier, all without being asked or expecting recognition for it.)

Ethel Turner wasn't alone. Her difficulties finding domestic help were part of a phenomenon known across the Western world as 'the servant problem'. The core of the problem was pretty simple – young women didn't want to be domestic servants any more. Who could blame them? The pay was bad, the hours were long and life in the average one-servant house could be lonely and isolated. Many of the girls were treated appallingly by their employers and, as servants, they were regarded as inferior.

But above all, there was the sheer drudgery of domestic service where they might work 16 hours a day at the beck and call of a demanding employer. Not surprisingly, girls preferred to work in shops and factories where they had friends to talk to, and they could clock on and off.

The sharp decline in servant numbers started around the turn of the century, and World War I was the final nail in the coffin. With the men away fighting, new job opportunities opened up for women and the live-in maid became a thing of the past.

The housework, meanwhile, was continuing to pile up, as it tends to do. By now it was obvious you couldn't pay someone to do it. The men didn't want to touch it. So what happened to all the domestic chores that used to be done by the live-in servant? They ended up on the shoulders of Australia's newest servant class – middle-class wives. (Working-class wives, of course, had always done their own housework.)

Science came to the rescue with a raft of labour-saving devices designed to ease the housewife's burden in the new era of servantless homes. Many of them – like the Twin Roller Mangle of 1908 – were scary-looking contraptions that still required a lot of hands-on physical labour to function. But even then, retailers were cottoning on to the phenomenon of the busy housewife. In 1913, Grace Bros. department store in Sydney was advertising a primitive washing machine called the Broadway Rotary Washer, manually operated, which promised half the labour of hand washing, 'in a third of the time'.

But it was the arrival of cheap electricity in the 1920s that really kicked off Australia's love affair with household appliances. Electric power was seen as the ultimate answer to the servant problem and all sorts of appliances became 'electric' with varying degrees of success. Some housewives began using the first electrical washing machines, which used a motor to agitate clothes and an electric wringer to squeeze the water out of them. (My grandmother was still using a later version of the old wringer machine when she died in 1975.)

For most working-class households, though, the new labour-saving devices were unaffordable, and would remain so for decades. The first big setback was the Great Depression, when jobs and money were scarce.

Tough times: housework in the 1930s

My father grew up in the 1930s, in poor rural areas in western NSW, where his father worked as a farm manager and labourer. As he recalls, housewives in the Depression made do with primitive appliances and could only dream of the new labour-saving devices available to the wealthy.

> *In my earliest years, we lived in tents in the bush and my mother cooked in a camp oven. This was a cast-iron pot buried in hot coals, in a hole in the ground. Bread, damper, meat, vegetables, cakes, all came out of it. The trick was to guess accurately just when things were 'done'. If something had to be boiled, it was done in a saucepan or billy over the open fire.*
>
> *When my father landed a job with a cottage attached, around 1934, we graduated to a wood-fired stove – the epicentre of domestic life back then. It warmed the house, cooked the meals, dried damp clothes, boiled the kettle, heated the flat-irons for 'doing up' the men's shirts, and toasted the bread.*
>
> *The main source of hot water, in better-off homes, was an appliance called a 'Fountain'. This was a large iron kettle with a tap on the front. If one kept the Fountain topped up, and the fire going in the stove, there was an endless supply of hot water. My mother longed for a Fountain, but it was a luxury she was never able to afford. We had a big kettle that served instead.*

Girls were raised for housework; that's just the way it was. Boys had chores, too. They brought in the firewood, rose first to light the stove and ran errands. On weekends, the men chopped the firewood; the women too, if their husbands forgot. The better-off hired others to do it for them – mostly Aborigines, but also the door-knocking unemployed.

There were fridges around before the war, but they were pretty primitive. Nearly everyone had an ice chest, into which the ice man deposited blocks of ice at sixpence a block. Then Edward Hallstrom brought out a kerosene-fired fridge called the 'Silent Knight' and made millions from it. The trouble with the early fridges was you had to keep up the kerosene or they just went out. They also had a tendency to catch fire.

The start of World War II signalled the end of the Depression, but there was still no relief in sight for housewives. Factories stopped their production of domestic items to focus on military needs, so women continued to do the housework the old-fashioned way – with lots of elbow grease, fuelled by regular cups of tea and neighbourly chats. Back then, as today, laundry was one of the most time-consuming tasks.

John Phillips and his father William near Condobolin, central west NSW, around 1934.

after
enlightenment,
the laundry

Zen proverb

Monday was washing day: the 1940s

Euleen Morse Stanford was one of 23 children from three marriages. Her mother's twelfth child, she grew up in the farming districts of north-western NSW. When Euleen was 18 months old her mother died suddenly and she was raised by her stepmother, May.

Everybody washed on a Monday. A woman's housework was judged by the whiteness of her washing, and it was there for everyone to see. We all had wire-netting fences, so of a Monday you could see everyone's washing hanging out all over town.

The women were up early, around 4.30 am, to light the copper. It was the kids' job to set it up the day before – chop the firewood, stack it underneath the copper and have it ready to go, so all May had to do was light the match. The copper was outside, with the washing benches set up under a shady tree. Sometimes the clothes were already in there, soaking overnight.

First in were the whites: the sheets, men's good shirts, tea towels and tablecloths. The soap powder went in at the same time. We used Rinso and Persil. As the clothes boiled, you'd poke them down with the wooden copper stick to keep them moving. How long was the stick? Long enough to keep a safe distance! You had to be darn careful because of the heat coming from the flames underneath the copper.

Once the whites were clean, you used the stick to lift them out onto the draining board – being careful because, of course, they were boiling hot – then transferred them into the tin rinsing tubs. The first one was clear water, to get the soap off, then they went into the second tub, which had a knob of Reckitt's Blue in it, to make the whites look really white.

Everything was wrung by hand before being hung on the line. The sheets were the hardest. They weighed a ton, wet. If there were two of you, you'd each grab an end and twist. It really was backbreaking work.

After the whites, you'd hand wash the colours on the scrubbing board with soap. Once the fire had gone out under the copper, the men's work clothes could sit in the hot water and soak. Then, when all that was over, we used that water for baths! Nothing went to waste.

Some women did their ironing the same day as the washing. They'd still be going late into the night, having started before sunrise. It was a long day.

By the time the war was over, there was a huge pent-up demand for domestic appliances. Factories started mass-producing household goods and, suddenly, things like washing machines, refrigerators and yes, the pressure cooker, were available to average Australian women.

A boom in credit meant that even poor people could buy them. As the 1950s ushered in a new era of stability and high employment, the craze for buying things on instalment, or time payment, swept the country. In 1957, a national retail campaign declared 'every woman deserves a washing machine' and many families happily went into debt to get one. For others, though, domestic life continued much as it had for decades.

The 1950s housewife

My mother, Gaye Phillips, was typical of her generation. She left school at 14 and worked as a secretary before marrying in her 20s. She raised four children in the 1950s and 60s, and remembers that many families got themselves into financial trouble buying household appliances on credit.

John and Gabrielle Phillips at Luna Park, around 1950.
'Your mother was very specific about wanting a Hawkins
pressure cooker when we got married. It was the very
latest thing.'

Everyone talks about the 1950s as a time of great prosperity in Australia, but really, a lot of people were very poor. Certainly there were plenty of good jobs – your father was a sales manager – but we still started out in the Housing Commission. In those days, a lot of people got into trouble using time payment for things like fridges. They'd get behind in their payments, then the fridge would be repossessed. There was a lot of talk about it in the papers. It was quite a scandal. [Prime Minister] Menzies came out and said, 'If people can't afford these things, they shouldn't buy them!'

We didn't want to get caught out, so the only thing we got on time payment was the lino in the lounge room and the two bedrooms. Instead of going into debt to buy a fridge, we had an ice box.

The most important appliance back then was the washing machine. It came before anything else, even a fridge. Our first place in West Heidelberg [in Melbourne] had a gas copper. That was in 1954. I was used to the wood-fired copper I'd grown up with in Queensland, so I thought the gas copper was a luxury. But it was still heavy work – you had to use the stick to get the washing out into the rinsing tubs, and you still had to wring by hand. That was a terrible job, especially with sheets. Women used to get big veins in their arms from it. Wringing by hand, everything took ages to dry.

Around 1958 I got a second-hand electric washing machine with an electric wringer on the top. That was a great advance, but the wringer was very dangerous. A neighbour got her long hair caught in it, and she was in a terrible state – it ripped her hair out by the roots, almost scalped her, because once she got caught, she couldn't reach the lever to turn it off. So you had to tie your hair back.

In the early 1960s I inherited a Hoover twin tub. Gosh, we thought we were made! It was only big enough to hold two towels and a sheet, but still, it was a lot better than using the wringer.

One tub was for washing, then you lifted it out and put it into the other tub for spinning. You could do the washing completely in one day, so it saved a lot of time. But a lot of people didn't like the twin tubs because they were so small, so that's when they came up with the automatic washing machines that we have today. But back then, only well-off people could afford them.

The credit boom of the 1950s left many older Australians with such a dread of personal debt and the evils of 'hire purchase' that to this day, many of them refuse to have a credit card. 'If you want something, save up for it and pay cash,' they told us.

Did we listen? Hell, no! Fifty years later, history would repeat itself. This time, it was schemes offering 'no interest, no repayments for 24 months!' that made the whole nation go credit-crazy. Once again, Australians were drowning in a sea of household debt, working harder and longer just to keep their heads above water. When the credit crunch hit in 2008, many of them would be wiped out.

Looking at the way our parents and grandparents lived gives us some fascinating clues as to how we've ended up in the mess we're in today. First, it shows that we don't learn from our mistakes, especially when it comes to buying things we can't afford. It shows that it's always been hard to get good household help. It shows that in the space of one or two generations we've experienced the most phenomenal social and technological changes in our history. My grandmother used to cook damper over hot coals in a hole in the ground; I can zap mass-produced frozen meals in a microwave. And that's within living memory. Incredible.

But most bizarrely of all, it shows that despite the social revolution, and all that whiz-bang technology, we're as time-stretched and exhausted as ever – just in different ways. The more things change, it seems, the more they stay the same.

Technology Versus Reality

So, do all our modern 'labour saving' devices actually reduce housework? The short answer is: no. But academics have been arguing about it for decades. The raging debate about housework illustrates just how difficult it's been for the boffins to get their clever heads around it – how to define it, how to measure it, and just how time-consuming it is.

It all started back in 1974, when sociologist Joann Vanek discovered that American women still spent the same amount of time doing housework as their grandmothers did, 50 years previously.[35] The tasks may have been different, but the workload was essentially the same – 53 hours of domestic work per week. Even Vanek agreed it didn't make sense – after all, modern housewives had plenty of labour-saving devices to help them, and a lot of them were also in the workforce.

So why hadn't their housework time decreased? Vanek's theory was that any time saved by the new domestic machines was neutralised by a number of other factors. As technology improved, domestic expectations increased. Housewives set the bar higher, aiming for cleaner houses, more elaborate meals, and clothes that were washed more frequently. In short, they became fussier and created more work for themselves.

More machines also meant more time buying, repairing and replacing them when they broke down (usually, in my experience, two days after their warranty expires). 'It's as if these labour-saving devices create their own work,' Vanek said.[36]

Vanek was criticised for her conclusions and other scientists set about disproving them, using different methods. They found the opposite: that the time women spent doing housework was

124

declining – and part of the reason was because of time-saving household appliances like dishwashers and microwaves.

With science divided over the issue, a group of Australian researchers tried to settle the argument once and for all – and found that Vanek was right. 'The analysis of this data shows that domestic technology rarely reduces women's unpaid working time and even, paradoxically, produces some increases in domestic labour,' they found. [37]

Their conclusion was that people use labour-saving devices to achieve ever-higher standards of cleanliness and refinement in their home, rather than free up time for other pursuits.

So now we know. Things like dishwashers and washing machines do not save us any time. They simply give us an incentive to wash even more dishes and more clothes.

The researchers, however, overlooked one small thing. There is one household appliance that saves time. One genuine labour-saving device that really does reduce the domestic workload. It's called a pressure cooker. But I've already mentioned that, right?

Secrets of a Desperate Housewife

Now we've established that housework is never-ending, everyone hates it, and there's virtually no machine that will reduce the time you spend doing it, what's the point of going on? As the Zen masters say: After enlightenment, the laundry. In other words, there's no getting out of it.

The good news is, there are ways to manage the domestic workload so it doesn't drain the life force out of you. You'll never be rid of the day-to-day necessity of it, but you can control it with a little forethought and organisation.

The golden rule of housework: declutter

The single most important thing you can do to reduce your housework is to declutter your home. Much of the work that goes into cleaning a house is caused not by actual dirt, but by 'stuff'. A messy, cluttered house full of stuff automatically appears dirty, whereas a tidy house with lots of space and light appears much cleaner than it actually is. So the more stuff you get rid of, the less housework you can get away with doing.

I am so enthusiastic about the benefits of decluttering (or purging, as I call it) that it is a regular part of my routine. A good purge – which usually involves taking a carload of toys and clothes to the local Red Cross shop – is the one domestic task I actually enjoy.

Sadly, decluttering does not come easily to everyone. It's one of life's little ironies that purgers are usually married to hoarders, who do not take kindly to having their beloved treasures 'disappeared' while their attention is elsewhere. And if you have two hoarders married to each other, then you're in real strife.

If decluttering is difficult for you, here are a few simple techniques to get you started.

- **Ease yourself into it** with the 'one in, one out' rule. Every time you buy an item, get rid of something equivalent. Extend this rule to other family members' possessions, especially children's: if they want a new toy, they need to say goodbye to an old one to free up the space. After a month, increase the ratio to 'one in, two out'. It'll take time, but you'll start seeing the mountain of mess diminishing.
- **Have a garage sale** once a year. Making money out of your stuff will ease the pain of parting with it. You'll also get greenie points for recycling your old trash, rather than adding it to landfill.
- **Open an eBay account** and start selling.

- **See it as an opportunity.** Once a month, get a black garbage bag and fill it with stuff for the local op shop. Be particularly ruthless with clothes. Remember the old adage that we wear 20 per cent of our clothes 80 per cent of the time. If you haven't worn an item of clothing in the past six months, get rid of it.
- **Tip it.** If you have a pile of junk unsuitable for the op shop, take it to the local tip. This was always one of my kids' favourite outings. In fact, once I even took a picnic so they could sit on the bonnet of the car and enjoy the sights and smells of the local tip while eating Vegemite sandwiches and sultanas.
- **If you live with a hoarder** who is particularly resistant to purging, quietly move the unwanted stuff into the garage. If they haven't noticed its absence after six months, get rid of it. Quickly.
- **Get help.** If the whole concept of decluttering is foreign to you and you don't know where to start, don't spend hundreds of dollars employing a professional decluttering expert. Any friend or relative with an evangelical zeal for decluttering will do the job just as well. Often it just takes a new pair of eyes.
- **Don't get caught up** in the nostalgia of 'stuff'. Memories are in your heart – not stuffed in a box in the cupboard. If you're surrounded by stuff that makes you dwell on pleasant times in the past, you're missing out on the present. Enjoy the here and now, be in the moment, and leave the past behind you!
- **Banish ornaments** – all they do is collect dust. Choose a couple of beautiful pieces, and a handful of favourite photographs, and put the rest away, out of sight. Rotate your favourite items rather than having them all on show at once. And if you're a collector of anything – teaspoons, plates on the wall, old dolls – I'm sorry, they have to go. Collection is just a respectable name for clutter.

The joy of storage

Storage runs a very close second to decluttering when it comes to making housework faster and more bearable. A good storage solution – like a good decluttering session – is guaranteed to make your heart sing and cut countless hours off a lifetime of cleaning and tidying.

- **Cull your possessions** ruthlessly, then make sure that whatever's left has a place, preferably out of sight. The aim is to have as many clear surfaces as possible – it makes cleaning a lot easier, and is visually more pleasant and calming.

- **Store it well.** These days there's a huge range of storage options available – if you're on a budget, try two-dollar shops, big discount stores like K-Mart, and the ever-reliable Ikea. If you've got more money to spend, there are specialist storage shops which also offer a consultation service.

- **'A place for everything,** and everything in its place'. The advantage of this is that everyone in the family knows where stuff goes – there's no excuse for leaving it lying around. Good storage makes it easier for everyone to pick up after themselves, lessening the load on the at-home partner.

- **Streamline your pantry** by using clear, airtight, plastic containers for all your dry goods (rice, pasta, breakfast cereal, etc). If you're short on cupboard space, put up some open shelves and store the containers there – they look great and are easier to access when cooking.

- **Store children's toys** in large plastic boxes with lids, preferably on low shelves where they are off the floor, but within reach of little people. Make it easy for your kids to understand what goes where – a box for Lego, another box for blocks, etc – then teach them from an early age to put their own toys away. Cull toys regularly. This is easier if you get the kids involved – ask them to choose which toys they would like to give away for other children to enjoy.

- **Look for clever storage solutions** that have a dual purpose, for example, seating cubes which can also be used to store DVDs, remotes and other lounge-room clutter. There are many beds available these days with storage underneath, and I've even seen a sofa that opens up to reveal a huge storage space underneath.
- **Junk the junk drawer.** The smallest but most lethal collector of clutter is the junk drawer. Every kitchen has one, filled with batteries, safety pins, matches and so on. Get rid of it forever by investing in a small set of plastic drawers which can fit inside a cupboard or on top of the fridge. Transfer the junk into the drawers (culling as you go, naturally), then label each drawer so you can access the items quickly.

How to clean your house in 12 minutes (or even less, depending how low your standards have dropped!)

- **Just use a fitted sheet** and a doona on beds instead of blankets and sheet sets. This makes it easier for children (and domestically challenged adults) to make their own beds. It's also much faster, and there's less to wash.
- **Reduce baby's mealtime mess** by placing a large sheet of plastic underneath the highchair. Unless they've got a particularly good arm, most of the mess should land on the plastic. Suck it up with a dustbuster and wipe the plastic clean at the end of the day. This will save you repeatedly sweeping, wiping and mopping.
- **Quick wash.** When the time comes to replace your washing machine, make sure you get one with the option of a 15-minute express wash. Otherwise, every load will take you an hour or more.
- **Only buy clothes** you don't have to iron, hand wash or dry-clean.
- **Reduce your laundry** mountain by only washing clothes when they need it. If it's still clean when you take it off, hang it up

in your wardrobe to be worn again – don't just toss it in the laundry hamper to save time. You'll cut your washing by up to 50 per cent immediately.

- **Working mothers, streamline** your professional wardrobe. Every year, I buy three pairs of black wash 'n' wear trousers, one pair of black summer shoes and one pair of black winter shoes (and if I find some I really like, I buy several identical pairs so I don't have to do it all again 12 months later). My bottom half is dressed exactly the same way five days a week, all year round. That way, the only wardrobe decision I have to make is what to wear on top. Believe me, it saves a lot of time. Fewer clothes mean less to store, less to pick up and less to launder.

    And if you think people will notice (or care) that you wear the same black trousers every day – they won't. In fact, performance artist Alex Martin wore the same brown dress every day for a year and nobody noticed. 'My take on that is that we're all too busy with our own appearance, family, work, etc to keep a tally on everyone else's wardrobe rotations,' she says. [38]

Chore Wars

What do you want first – the good news or the bad? There's plenty of both on the long road to domestic democracy.

The good news is that Australian women are doing less housework than 40 years ago, and men are doing twice as much as they used to. For women, though, it's only one hour less per week (bad news). And since men were doing very little to start with, doubling their contribution hasn't actually made much difference (more bad news). But at least they do more than Japanese men (hoorah!).[39]

Both men and women spend more time caring for their children than they did 20 years ago (good news). For men, though, that equates to about a minute a day during the week (bad news) and for women, it's meant sacrificing sleep, leisure, washing and grooming to allow for it (bad news for personal hygiene).[40]

There are more academic studies on this subject that you can poke a broomstick at. But the results vary so wildly, and are based on so many different criteria, that it's hard to draw anything but general conclusions. In general, men work longer hours in the workforce, but women work longer overall because, as well as their paid jobs, they do the bulk of the domestic work.

So what's the solution? In the long-term, a change in attitudes and workplace practices are the only things that will sort out the domestic divide. In the short-term, here are my top four Fair Share Hints for a more democratic division of housework.

Hint 1: Just don't do it

Not as silly as it sounds. Men are genetically gifted at this technique and women are gradually getting the hang of it. Studies show that as women increase their paid work they reduce the amount of housework they do and lower their standards. Over time, many of the routine domestic tasks done by our mothers and grandmothers – the 'senseless tyranny of spotless shirts and immaculate floors'[41] – have become redundant, all but disappearing in the space of a generation.

Take ironing. I was recently chatting with a couple of senior female colleagues at the ABC (about children and housework, naturally) and one mentioned that her mother-in-law had come to visit.

'The first thing my husband does is ask his mum to iron some shirts for him,' she said. 'He wouldn't dare ask me, of course. But she loves it! She gets the ironing board out in a flash. She even asks him if he wants a crease ironed in his jeans.'

'Who irons jeans these days?' said the other colleague.

'Who irons anything?' I asked. 'You just put your clothes on and walk around in them for a bit. It's called body heat.'

Obviously there are many domestic tasks without which civilised life would disintegrate. But there are plenty of others, like scrubbing the shower recess, which can simply be ignored indefinitely without the world collapsing. (Note to editor: no need to footnote this conclusion. Tested and proved by author over many years).

As effective as this technique is, it's not always easy for high-achieving perfectionists who typically struggle most with the dirt and chaos inherent in the work/family juggle. For them, I suggest listening to the scientists, who tell us that red wine is good for the heart, and that parents obsessed by cleanliness are weakening their children's immune systems, exposing them to chronic illnesses like asthma and eczema.

The clear scientific message is: skip the kids' baths for a few nights and pour yourself a big glass of red instead. It works for me!

Hint 2: Pay someone else to do it

Post-children, there are few experiences more joyful than coming home to a spotless house that you haven't cleaned yourself. Having a cleaner is a delicious luxury that I've indulged in, off and on over the past six years, whenever finances permit. But the idea that the whole housework issue can be resolved by having somebody come in for a few hours a week is a nonsense.

'Why don't more couples pay to have their houses cleaned? That's one of the great mysteries in the modern household today,' wrote Bettina Arndt in *The Canberra Times*.[42] 'In Australia, most women prefer to soldier on alone, wallowing in their domestic martyr status and bitching about unhelpful husbands.'

Arndt – who in a previous newspaper article wrote that fathers work harder than mothers, and the whole housework debate is a con-job [43]– suggested that all those whining women should just pay for a cleaner and be done with it.

Arndt was clearly suffering a touch of the Marie Antoinettes: 'The women are revolting, m'lady!' 'Then let them hire servants!' So I emailed her to update her on the real world. The reason more couples do not hire cleaners, I told her, is very simple – they cost $35 an hour.

Even if couples can afford $150 a week to have a cleaner come in for a few hours (and very few can in the current climate), it represents only a tiny proportion of the domestic work. Once the cleaner goes home, there's still another 40 to 50 hours of shopping, cooking, cleaning, laundry and childcare left to do. Who does that? Not the housework fairy, last time I checked.

Having a cleaner is a drop in the ocean. But as luxuries go, it beats a Hermès handbag any day.

Hint 3: Make it illegal for spouses not to do their fair share

Attractive, but highly unlikely. While Australian governments are happy to interfere in certain aspects of people's private lives (ad campaigns telling them to exercise, eat vegetables and stop smoking, for example), they are so far reluctant to march into suburban kitchens and legislate on the cooking and washing.

As fanciful as the idea sounds, though, there is a precedent. Spain has introduced a clause in the civil marriage contract obliging men to share the domestic load, including taking care of children and elderly relatives. Failure to do so will be taken into account when deciding divorce settlements.

It's too early to say whether it will have any impact on the behaviour of Spanish husbands. Maybe it's just symbolic, not practical. But like Australia's tentative move to give new fathers two weeks' paid parental leave, it shows that governments are starting to acknowledge that men, too, have domestic responsibilities and families they'd love to see more of. 'There is a high value placed on family care in Australia. Everyone's doing their best,' social researcher Lyn Craig told *The Australian* newspaper. 'It's just a case of developing policies to help men assist.' [44]

Hint 4: Have the argument

Unpleasant as it is, having The Argument about housework is often the only truly effective way to sort it out. The argument can go on for years. At times, it can get very nasty. It can cause otherwise happy couples to doubt the very basis of their relationship. It may seem futile and never-ending. But it's my firm belief that there's no avoiding it. You have to have the argument.

The important thing about the housework argument is that it's not really about housework. It's about fairness and respect. It's not fair for one person to come home from work and put their feet up for the rest of the day while their partner comes home from work and carries on working. It is not respectful to regard a spouse as a domestic servant and personal valet, albeit a high-ranking and valued one. It's insulting.

It's also about taking responsibility for tasks, not just doing them reluctantly when directed by an irate partner for the 50th time. Taking responsibility for household chores means recognising they exist, remembering they need to be done, organising the materials you need to carry them out and making them a priority in your schedule, often sacrificing all those fun things you'd much rather be doing. Not just once. Every day. Year after year. Until the day you cark it, in fact, without anybody noticing and giving you a gold star. Boring, but true.

So what, exactly, is a fair split of the responsibilities? For starters, it's not necessarily equal. Splitting domestic chores 50/50 is unrealistic or impractical for most couples. Studies show that Australian women generally have very low expectations of what their partners will contribute, and are usually satisfied with something far less than equitable.[45] Fair is whatever the two parties perceive to be fair. If you're both happy with the deal, then it's a fair deal. If one party's not happy with the deal, then ... you have to have the argument.

Most people will do anything to avoid conflict. They don't want to expose their children to it and they don't want to cause problems in their marriage. But not having the argument about housework is far more damaging in the long run. Simmering resentment and unexpressed anger are guaranteed to kill a marriage. Regular bouts of robust communication, on the other hand, may well be its best chance of survival.

Fighting the good housework fight does, of course, carry inherent risks. Constant bickering over seemingly trivial matters is hard on a relationship, especially when there are so many other pressures. But my own experience is that the argument about housework does not go on forever. Two people who care about each other's happiness and want their family to stay intact will reach an agreement.

For us, the argument about housework and childcare led to an unusual resolution, one that would turn the traditional family structure on its head and test just about every prejudice and gender stereotype we both possessed.

We called it The Great Role Reversal Experiment.

men make
very good
mothers.
seriously.

Boris Cyrulnik, French psychoanalyst [46]

family

Everyone does it tough when they're juggling work and kids. Everyone. It's easy to look around and think other people are managing so much better than you are. Trust me, they're not. Everybody struggles, and everybody puts on a brave face. The most supportive thing you can do for yourself, and others, is to stop pretending you're perfect.

family

WHEN WE FIRST EMBARKED on The Great Role Reversal Experiment we had no idea what we were in for. Why would we? We were entering uncharted waters. We didn't know one other family where the mother was the main breadwinner and the father the primary child-carer. And judging by the reactions we got, it soon became apparent that nobody else knew such a family either.

No wonder.

The average Australian family these days is one where dad works full-time and mum works part-time. Becoming less common (but far from extinct) are the traditional male-breadwinner, mum-at-home families, where the old 1950s way of doing things works best, especially when the kids are little. But coming up hot on their heels are the dual-income families, where both mum and dad work full-time and argue a lot over whose turn it is to fold the washing.

Then you've got the idealistic mob at sharedparenting.com, who believe that a 50/50 split in childcare, housework, bread-winning and recreational time is actually achievable. You've got single parents doing it all on their own, families where there are two mums or two dads, and divorced parents who divide it up depending on their level of animosity or whatever the courts have decided.

And then, sitting in the corner looking quite lonely, you've got the rarest species of all – the Role Reversers. These families have turned the predominant modern structure on its head by having mum work full-time as the main breadwinner, with dad at home looking after the kids and doing part-time or freelance work to supplement the household income.

There's statistical evidence that these families are gradually becoming more common – in just two years, the number of families with a dad at home full-time jumped 35 per cent. But they're still so rare that they barely register on the graph. In 2008, there were 12 000 stay-at-home dads in Australia, compared to 230 000 stay-at-home mums. [47] That is, about one in 20 families either choose, or are forced, to do things this way. 'I know one bloke in our area, but before that I'd never come across any,' stay-at-home dad Matthew told ABC Radio 720 Perth in April 2008. [48]

Our decision to join this tiny percentage of the population was based purely on finances and practicality. In an ideal world, neither of us would have chosen it. Quite frankly, it was the last resort. As Mario explained it to a friend, 'Mate, I can't afford to work!' Financially, we needed my salary to pay the bills. But practically – because of my odd hours and the long distance we lived from the city – we needed someone at home to be with the children. We didn't want our kids to be raised by nannies and in any case, we couldn't afford it. Plus, there was the housework. With both of us working, we spent most of our time arguing about who should do it. We had no choice. The only logical, workable solution was to switch roles.

From day one, role reversal was a battle: against our own prejudices, and against everyone else's.

For starters, other people just didn't get it. No matter how patiently we explained that I was the main breadwinner and Mario was the primary carer, it didn't seem to register. I was the one people automatically deferred to on any matter involving the children. I was 'the mother'. The act of giving birth, it seemed, had made me the world expert on our children. Government letters regarding immunisation and childcare issues were addressed to me. Doctors and child health nurses spoke only to me, even when both of us were present. The preschool rang me if there was a problem. At parks and playgrounds, other mothers struck up conversations with me. Mario was usually ignored.

The reaction of other people, in fact, was one of the biggest challenges we encountered. No matter how hard we tried to settle in to our new roles, we came up against a brick wall of society's resistance on a daily basis.

For me, the constant pressure to fulfil the traditional maternal role, as well as that of family breadwinner, was close to unbearable. Logistically, it was impossible to do it all. Nonetheless, in the early days I tried, because the guilt of not doing it all – of being the bad mother, the selfish career woman – was worse.

It was particularly noticeable once Marcus started preschool. I felt horribly guilty that, unlike many other school mums, I was rarely available to do my bit. I had no time to join the parent council (which was really the mothers' council), no time to organise play dates, no time to join the regular coffee mornings where friendships were formed.

At the same time, it irked me that all the expectation fell on the mothers, while the dads were assumed to be too busy working to be able to contribute much. Nobody would have dreamed of asking the school dads to bake three different types of cakes and biscuits for the school fete, or to stand outside the local supermarket for hours selling raffle tickets. Yet it was assumed that the mothers – many of whom worked at least part-time – were both available and willing to do it.

It really hit home when I overheard two of the mothers discussing how school parents fell into two camps – those who pulled their weight and those who didn't. I slunk away like a pariah and didn't show my face at the gate for a month.

For Mario, the assumptions about parental roles were equally annoying. He no longer had the public recognition that came with a successful career and his new domestic role wasn't recognised either. 'What does he actually do all day?' asked a female acquaintance, an at-home mum, in an amused tone. 'He does what you do,' I snapped. 'Just without the coffee mornings.' That shut her up.

Of course, that wasn't strictly true. An at-home dad doesn't do the same things an at-home mum does. Any working mother who arrives home from a hard day at the office expecting a spotless house, freshly bathed children and a glass of wine waiting is bound to be disappointed. She may, however, find that a retaining wall's been built, the rabid possum's been evicted from the roof, and the kids suddenly know how to play tennis.

That's the first thing you learn about role reversal – it's not a straightforward swap of breadwinning and caring roles. It's more like chucking the whole lot into the air and each person doing what they can, depending on time and circumstances.

Men and women do things differently. Not better, not worse. Just – very differently.

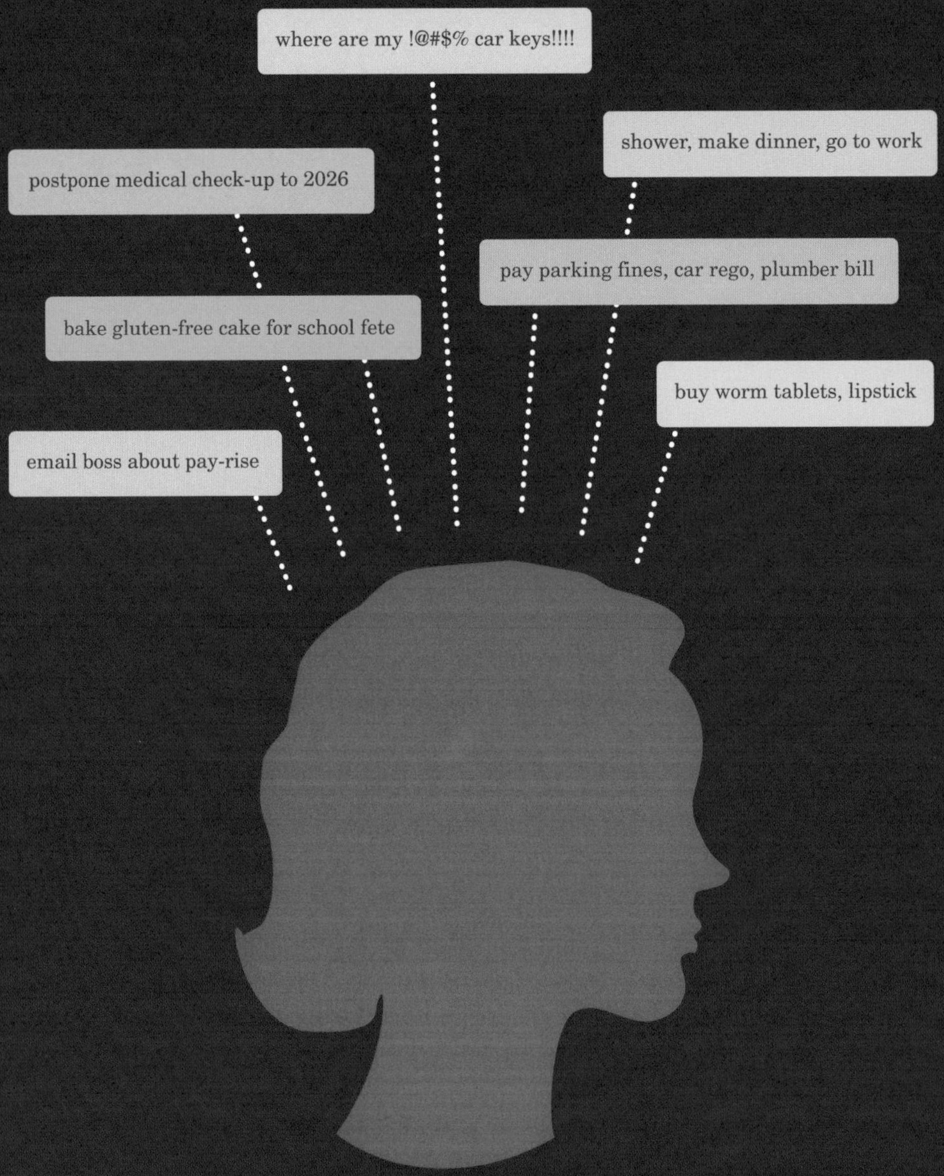
where are my !@#$% car keys!!!!
shower, make dinner, go to work
postpone medical check-up to 2026
pay parking fines, car rego, plumber bill
bake gluten-free cake for school fete
buy worm tablets, lipstick
email boss about pay-rise

TOP JOB CAREER WIFE

● The exceptionally successful career wife is a modern product whose status brings a complex train of marriage problems.

THERE is the minor problem of overwork versus boredom, which for most wives means facing the new eternal triangle of not the other woman but the strenuous three - part demands of husband, children, and career.

One of the talents expected of the new career women is the ability to have two personalities, both equally effective.

The forceful, shrewd, enterprising executive Miss H. at the office must become a good deal cosier when she steps back into her married life at the end of the day, if she is to keep the home fires burning.

We recall the case history of the successful business woman who made the man she married into her business partner. All day long she took the right decisions, he carried them out, and the firm's business boomed.

Two years of this, and at the end of the day he put on his hat and took another girl out to dinner.

There is also the problem of "dehuffing." Any woman with enough money to be financially independent may have to face the awkward problem of dehuffing the man in her life. This kind of huff is utterly unpredictable and can blow up on the most inconsequential issue.

It cannot be exorcised entirely, no matter what spell you cast on him, but there are certain extra security measures for keeping a husband out of a huff. They are by no means infallible, but some women we know use them with success.

They avoid too-frequent reference to being financially independent, any laying down of the law in front of other people, any lone-wolf behaviour on decisions that would affect both of them, any supplanting of "our" by "my," and too many attempts to push into his province the domestic jobs which he considers to be her chore.

Mollifying tactics include any cash payment towards an item he would normally pay the lot on, and an extra show of consideration for his domestic tastes ("my husband doesn't care for marrow so we never have it") to quell his suspicion that she is too wrapped up in her career.

The hardest part of the problem is that when she puts so much energy into a job and a home the place that it shows is her face.

By
ANNE EDWARDS
and
DRUSILLA BEYFUS

THE AUSTRALIAN WOMEN'S WEEKLY — April 24, 1957

The Good Old, Bad Old Days

Managing family life was all so much simpler 50 years ago. Men went out to work, women stayed at home and everyone knew the rules. 'Your father used to give me the housekeeping money each week and I was in charge of how it was spent,' Mum tells me. 'He never interfered because that was my area. He had his, I had mine. Nowadays, everyone wants a say in everything. It seems very complicated.'

It's easy to look back at that era with rose-coloured glasses. In fact, the whole Domestic Goddess revival owes a lot to our nostalgia for it. Today's young women are baking and knitting up a storm. Department stores sell retro-style Mixmasters for $800 a pop, and according to a survey by *The Daily Telegraph*, a staggering 70 per cent of working mothers would rather be at home full-time with their children.[49]

But would they really? There were good reasons why the old ways failed, and why women left the kitchen and stormed into the workforce as soon as they had the opportunity. The answer is not to scurry back in there when the going gets tough. The answer is to find some balance.

The fact is, there's a lot of joy to be had caring for the people you love and creating a comfortable, harmonious home. And there's also a lot of joy to be had from a successful career and financial independence. Without both, many of us find that life seems to be missing something. But when you have too much of everything – as I realised during my on-air choking fit – it's a catastrophe.

The Birth of Superwoman

So where did this whole ridiculous idea come from, that women can have it all, simultaneously, without paying a terrible price? The early feminists swear blind it wasn't their idea – they just wanted women to have choice. Maybe we can blame Shirley Conran – at least for naming the phenomenon and turning it into a bestseller. In 1975, she released the book *Superwoman*, in which she coined the famous phrase 'life's too short to stuff a mushroom'. The book became a bible for a generation of newly liberated women, and 'superwoman' became the ideal they aspired to. Conran's solution to juggling career and family was to cut corners with the housework. If there was dirt on the floor, she advised that you sweep it under the rug. Or pay another woman to do it. (The concept that housework might be anything other than a woman's responsibility was still light years away. That was superwoman's downfall.)

Before long, superwoman was part of the vernacular, a mythical figure of monstrous proportions. Also known as 'supermum', she effortlessly raised multiple children, ran the house and had a high-flying career in a male-dominated field. All while looking gorgeous and maintaining her composure.

Allegedly.

One of Australia's original superwomen was Quentin Bryce, now our first female Governor-General. Back in the 1970s and '80s, she was the epitome of the 'have it all/do it all' generation – Queensland's first female barrister, a feminist activist and mother of five. (Yes, five children.)

But behind her impeccably groomed facade, Quentin Bryce, like most superwomen, was struggling to hold it together.

In 2004, during a speech at a mental health conference, she revealed how close she came to a nervous breakdown when she was in her mid-20s. 'I had three children under four. I was working full-time and I had neglected my health. I remember lying in my bed, shrouded in fear, asking myself how would I ever cope with my little baby, two

toddlers, keeping my household running, my job, my marriage, my life …
I had heard and read about breakdowns. Suddenly I had a glimpse,
and an unforgettable one, of what the word means.' [50]

Superwoman drops dead of exhaustion, aged 34

If someone like Quentin Bryce had trouble doing it all, no wonder
other women threw in the towel.

After peaking during the 1990s, the superwoman myth started
to lose its lustre. A study by Cambridge University in 2008 found
support for the whole idea had been waning steadily, with both men
and women concerned that family life was suffering.[51] As the world
entered the new millennium, superwoman was in her death throes.
'Opinions are shifting as the shine of the supermum wears off,' said
Professor Jacqueline Scott, the study's author. 'The idea of women
juggling high-powered careers while also baking cookies and reading
bedtime stories is increasingly seen to be unreasonable by ordinary
mortals.'

And Shirley Conran? Having popularised the superwoman ideal,
she too moved on from the idea of women doing everything. In 2000,
she founded the Work/Life Balance Trust in the UK, aimed at creating
greater equality in the workplace, and 'domestic democracy' at home.

Ghost of superwoman

But as I discovered, you can't kill superwoman off that easily. Like
that other horror from the 1980s – shoulder pads – she keeps rising
from the grave and haunting us. It was my failed attempt to be
superwoman/supermum that pushed us into role reversal in the first
place. And even then, I carried on trying. It took several years before
I finally accepted how pointless and damaging it was – and that was
the day that role reversal finally started working for us.

Dropping the quest to be perfect is one of the key factors to successfully juggling work and family. But even though most of us know, in theory, that having it all and doing it all is fraught with danger, the pressure to keep trying is enormous. Read any women's magazine and you could be forgiven for thinking superwoman lives on. She's had a bit of plastic surgery, and she's usually rich and famous, but it's undeniably her. Or more precisely, it's a mob of celebrities pretending to be superwomen and in the process making real women everywhere feel like failures.

I personally know of several high-profile Australian women who actively promote a public image of themselves as 'ordinary working mums', combining busy careers with looking after their young children. I also happen to know they have full-time nannies – a fact that mysteriously never emerges during publicity interviews.

Magazine and newspaper articles about them invariably contain quotes along the following lines: 'Like all working mums, I sometimes find it difficult to juggle everything, but the most important thing in my life is being with my children. They come first. If it was a choice between my kids and my career, I'd give it up this minute. They bring me so much joy and they make the struggle all worth it. I didn't have children so that somebody else can look after them.' (And where was the nanny during all this – in the cupboard?)

The invisible nanny is also popular with Hollywood supermums like Angelina Jolie (who presumably has a team of them working shifts), and Posh Beckham, who reportedly makes hers walk several metres behind her in public so she doesn't spoil the paparazzi shots of mum and kids.

There's obviously nothing wrong with a busy person employing someone to help – successful men have armies of them – so why the secrecy? Maybe women are just embarrassed. Paying someone else to look after your children is still seen by many people as a failing. I don't believe these celebrity 'superwomen' deliberately conceal it but by omission, they give the impression they're doing it all themselves, fuelling the superwoman myth and making normal mothers feel like failures.

You can understand why, though. Mothers who work full-time already attract more than their fair share of disapproval, and they're blamed for all sorts of social ills, from fat kids to the high rate of divorce. Women who are successful to boot arouse even more suspicion. For such a woman to admit that she pays somebody to take care of her children invites a whole range of hurtful judgements: you're selfish, you're pampered, you treat your kids like an accessory, you've sacrificed your children's happiness for your career. Not to mention the most toxic of all: why bother having kids if you don't want to spend every waking minute with them? (Nobody ever asks fathers that question, incidentally.)

No wonder they hide the nanny in the cupboard when journalists come knocking.

There are exceptions, though. When I interviewed Sarah Murdoch for *The Bulletin*, she was up-front about employing a nanny. Initially she said she'd been uncomfortable about it, because her own mother had raised her family with no help at all. Despite her enormous wealth and fame, Murdoch was determined to be a hands-on mum herself. But with her charitable work and business taking up more and more time, it was her mother who convinced her there was nothing wrong with having someone help with the children if you could afford it. 'I would have!' she told her daughter.

CNN's famous war correspondent Christiane Amanpour was similarly candid. A few months after giving birth to her son, Amanpour was back reporting in the world's hot-spots. I asked how she managed to do it. 'We have very good help,' she said with characteristic bluntness. 'Lots of it.'

The moral of the story is this: there's no shame in asking for help. And there's no shame in paying for it, either.

As Antonia Kidman wrote about motherhood: 'As long as women … disguise reality with a facade of perfection, they stop themselves moving forward. Sometimes honesty and vulnerability can be the most enlightening tools of all.'[52]

Which Brings Us Back to Role Reversal …

The death of the superwoman myth has left modern families with the mother of all dilemmas: how do you juggle childcare, housework and financial responsibilities with the career aspirations of the two individuals who hold it all together?

In families where the father earns more money, it's reasonably straightforward. The decisions aren't that difficult and the status quo prevails. But in the growing number of Australian families where the mother's earning potential is equal to, or greater than, the father's, the possibility of role reversal is one that needs to be considered and supported.

The big question is: does it work?

The answer, for us, has been: Yes. No. Sort of. Sometimes.

Yes, it's worked, because we've been able to give our children a stable home and financial security. No, it hasn't worked, because for six years there's been a lot of arguments about who does what.

It's worked for me because, unlike most women, my career is still intact despite having children – and in television, that's almost unheard of. But it hasn't worked for me because I'm always tired and I hardly see my kids except at weekends. Most of the time, I feel like a machine: a no-maintenance domestic and corporate robot who diligently services the needs of others. The woman I used to be – the one who laughed, cried, acted the goat, slacked off, was excited by stuff – has gone missing.

It's worked for Mario because he's had time with his children that most modern dads would envy. When the kids have a nightmare, it's Dadda they call for – not me. But it hasn't worked for him, because his career's been pretty well skewered. The loss of identity has hit him hard. Harder, I suspect, than it hits women who've been psychologically prepped for it their whole life.

> *We tried it [role reversal] for six months after I had my daughter, because I was earning more money. But it didn't work for us. I'd get home from work, and – well, dinner would sometimes be cooked – but it was all the little things that wouldn't be done. Bathing the baby, tidying up, the washing. I'd come home to that, then be up all night breastfeeding, then get up and go to work again. I was just too tired. And it wasn't good for my husband emotionally. It just didn't work.*
> Lucia, mother-of-two, journalist

So Why Do It?

I'm treading carefully here. Personally, I have found role reversal to be extremely difficult and, given the choice, I wouldn't do it. I cannot speak for Mario and he has decided, after careful consideration, not to write about his experience of role reversal for this book. It's still a touchy subject for us.

At the same time, there are lots of positives and I would hate to discourage anyone from at least giving it a go. Yes, it's stressful juggling work and family this way; but it's stressful juggling work and family however you do it. And reversing the traditional roles – or at least, giving them a good shake-up – has a lot going for it, for both partners. In today's world, it's a viable option.

So let's look at the pluses. For me, the number one benefit of our role-reversal experiment has been the relationship between the children and their father. It's not that they love each other more than other kids and dads do, or that they have a better relationship. It's just that they've had the time to enjoy their relationship, explore it, become bored with it. There's no yearning there, no 'father hunger'. They take their love for each other completely for granted. They're immersed in it, 24/7. And that's been a joyful thing to witness. Even at the toughest times, it has lightened my heart and brought tears to my eyes to see the three people I care most about in the world enjoying the gift of time together. We are very, very lucky – and so are our children – that we've had that father-time to offer them. For better and worse, they know each other inside out.

Role reversal has also taught me to appreciate the different skill-set that Mario brings to parenting. This did not happen immediately. In fact, for the first couple of years it was the differences that drove me mad. I didn't want Mario to parent the children his way. I wanted him to parent them my way. I wanted them to be fed every night at 5.30 pm, bathed at 6 pm and in bed by 7 pm. I wanted their clothes washed and dried and folded and put away, all on the same day, not over a two-week period. I felt the children should be the centre of our existence, and that our day should revolve around equal parts of recreation, education and green vegetables. I wanted order, routine, and yes, dammit, I wanted to come home to a clean house.

The thing that shocked me most was how patriarchal I became. All of the sexist traditions I had scoffed at as a single woman became strangely attractive once I became the main breadwinner. I felt entitled to a fair bit of domestic support because I was earning the money, and when it didn't work out that way, I obsessed night and day about the unfairness of it all. I knew it was wrong – after all, I wouldn't want to spend my whole life doing housework and changing nappies, so why should Mario? I knew full well that going into the office was a lot easier than looking after a baby and a toddler while trying to work from home. But I couldn't stop the mean little voice inside my head telling me otherwise.

At the same time as whingeing about the housework, I also clung jealously to it as my area of expertise. As well as being a 1950s patriarchal chauvinist, I was also, it turned out, that other horrible thing – a martyr. I was good at eye-rolling, sighing and explosive utterances such as, 'Oh for God's sake, just leave it! I'll do it.'

In particular, I guarded the washing machine like an Alsatian, convinced that the moment my back was turned Mario would throw a red sock in with the whites and the whole world would collapse. He repeatedly asked me to teach him how to use the pressure cooker, and I repeatedly found excuses not to. The nasty little voice in my head encouraged me: 'He won't do it properly. He'll forget it's on the stove and your lovely pot will be ruined.' In retrospect, I was my own worst enemy. And his, come to think of it.

Luckily for all of us, Mario had no intention of rolling over and doing things my way. The more I tried to enforce my vision of the perfect family, the more he dug his heels in. If the kids were having a good time, he'd keep them at the park until after dark and bundle them into bed in their clothes. He saw no reason why they should be entertained 24/7 and they quickly learned to be patient while he took them around hardware stores and into the college.

Meanwhile, fluff was building up under the sofa and I seemed to be the only one who cared.

At first, I found the lack of routine infuriating. But as time went on, I had to admit – begrudgingly – that Mario was very good at wrangling the kids. Much better than me. When he told them to do something, they did it without a murmur. When I told them to do something, they'd look sideways at each other and burst out laughing. If the children left toys on the floor, Mario threw them in the rubbish bin – literally. They quickly learned to pick up after themselves. I realised he had the discipline thing sorted, while I'd missed the boat completely. The kids twigged I was a pushover even before I did. I realised it the day Marcus informed his little sister: 'Let's have a treat. Mamma's rules are different from Dadda's rules.'

One night, I came home to find that Mario had moved a small bookcase into the kitchen and set up the children's plates, cutlery and cereal on it. 'They're going to make their own breakfast from now on,' he announced. 'Even Mischa.' I was dismayed. 'She's only two! She'll make a mess.' But Mario insisted. The children, he said, needed to feel capable and independent. A bit of mess was a small price to pay.

The next morning, the children dressed themselves (another Mario reform) and rushed downstairs, squealing joyfully with anticipation. They were thrilled by the huge responsibility of making their own breakfast and, to my astonishment, they managed it without too much mishap. Within a week, they were pouring the milk, spooning on yoghurt, and cutting a banana into slices with virtually no assistance. Afterwards, they took their plates to the sink, then cleaned the table.

I was impressed, not only with them, but with Mario. According to the experts, he was right: sharing domestic duties can help a child's development.

'As long as the whole family is involved, even preschoolers can be designated tasks around the house,' clinical psychologist Amanda Frawley told *Sunday Life* magazine. 'These activities can teach them a sense of responsibility as well as introducing the idea of a positive work ethic.'[53]

As a journalist, I was the one who read all this stuff in the papers. But at home, if it had been left to me, I would have happily spoon-fed the kids for years because it was quicker and easier.

Mario wasn't an obsessive reader like I was, but he seemed to know these things instinctively. It wasn't just issues of discipline and responsibility, either – he spent hours teaching the children how to draw and paint, whereas I quickly became bored. He discovered that the best way to stop them squabbling on long car trips was to play classical music and get them to make up a story to go with it. At bedtime, he ditched the usual fairy tales and introduced them to guided meditation. If they cried during the night, he was nearly always the one who went to them.

When the time came for Mischa to stop wearing nappies at night, our GP advised us to wait until summer, then ease her into it with pull-ups. Nonsense, decided Mario. He had a long, private talk with Mischa, and walked her through the journey from her bed to the toilet. From that night on, she slept without a nappy, and has never wet the bed once.

The realisation that Mario was good at parenting – better, in many ways, than I was – was a blow to my pride. But it also forced me to examine my whole approach to role reversal, and the preconceived ideas I'd brought into it. Maybe he had a point about the housework – maybe it wasn't that important if the house was a bit messy and dirty, and if he forgot to return the videos. That was his responsibility and his problem, I realised – he was a smart man, let him figure it out. Gradually, I stopped hovering and instructing and realised that the sky hadn't fallen in after all. I noticed, in fact, that the more I let go, the better things worked. Without my saying a word, washing was folded and dishes were done. Not always. But enough.

My initial impatience with Mario as he struggled to learn new skills has changed to admiration and respect. It takes a lot of guts for a man to stay at home with his kids while his wife goes out to work. As the at-home dad told ABC Radio, the experience is 'not for everybody. You've got to be patient, but you've also got to be confident to take your child into those situations where you're surrounded by women in unfamiliar circumstances. You've got to … have a strong enough personality to overcome those barriers.'[54]

Most men, I suspect, would flat out refuse to do it. While women derive obvious benefits from role reversal – less housework and an uninterrupted career – men have to look a lot harder to see what's in it for them.

It's taken us several years, but we're finally getting the hang of it. Role reversal may not be the easiest road to take, but – after threatening to tear us apart – it has taught us both valuable lessons and, in many ways, brought us closer together. I've long given up the dream of having a perfectly neat, clean house, and to be honest, it's a relief. As I've relaxed and discovered my inner slob, Mario's picked up the slack, confident that he's not going to be criticised for the result.

And the ultimate test of role reversal? The kids are happy. We're still together. There's still a big pile of fluff underneath the sofa. And that's okay.

Nicole's story

Nicole and her husband Matt tried role reversal for 12 months after their first baby was born, for virtually the same reasons as Mario and I did. Even though they ultimately decided role reversal was not for them, it's interesting that their experience of it was very similar to ours. For Matt, the main issue was the isolation and lack of support he felt as an at-home dad; for Nicole, the main issue was housework.

After Maya's birth, we didn't like the idea of putting her into full-time daycare and we couldn't afford a nanny. I had the higher income so the plan was for me to work full-time and Matt would do some casual bar work. He wanted to bond with his daughter, plus he thought it would be great to stay at home and have a break after working full-time.

Adjusting to the change of roles was more difficult than we expected. The bar work turned out to be Matt's release from the stresses of fatherhood and marriage. He started going out partying after work, then trying to catch up on sleep during the day when the baby slept. He was exhausted, nothing was getting done around the house and he was becoming depressed. He started to feel emasculated. People didn't show him much respect as a stay-at-home dad and I was nagging him about getting the housework done.

He was also feeling lonely as the primary child-carer. None of our friends had that arrangement and he had little support. He started having cocktail hour at home by himself in the afternoons.

I wasn't happy with the situation either. Even though I was working full-time I was still doing the majority of the cleaning and laundry at home. Before I left for work, I'd make sure all the meals were prepared. And I was still breastfeeding through the night. Meanwhile, Matt would be having these great days out with Maya, catching trains and ferries and basically just having fun, without having to do all the boring domestic stuff.

That's how it felt to me, anyway.

It was a difficult time because I was pleased to be out of the house with a purpose, but Matt was really struggling. No-one took his role as main carer seriously. He also found out how difficult it is staying at home with a baby, how demanding and emotionally draining it can be. His depression and the impact on our relationship was significant.

The pressure lifted when we found out I was pregnant again. Knowing that he would return to the role of main breadwinner made him much happier.

Our role reversal lasted 12 months, but to be honest, it just didn't work for us. There were a couple of positives – a chance for me to continue my career, plus Matt developed a great bond with our daughter.

Right now, I'm expecting our third child. Matt works full-time, and I work part-time. He's comfortable with the breadwinner role and his self-esteem has returned. I still do the majority of the housework, but he cooks on the days I work and 'tidies' the house on Saturdays. I still worry about the washing, the shopping, the bills, doctor's visits, planning ahead, holidays, day care. That part annoys me.

Overall, I think our family would work most successfully with both parents sharing part-time work and parenting. (Actually, a live-in nanny/housekeeper would solve all my problems, but of course that would never be affordable!)

Once number three arrives, it looks like I will have to stay at home full-time. I'm dreading the thought, but I don't feel I have any choice. A mother is a mother – it's a job you can't really change, no matter what you do.

Surviving the Work/Family Juggle

Since I became a mother, I've spoken to hundreds of working parents and quizzed them at length about how they manage the juggle. In return, I've been asked similar questions myself. It's like there's this enormous secret society of stressed parents out there, all sidling up to each other, asking: 'So, ah ... how do you do it?'

Over the years, those countless conversations at the water cooler and the school gates have yielded many gems of wisdom that have helped me through. Most can be boiled down to a few simple realities.

1 **Hang in there** Things do get better. The toughest time for anybody to be working is when they have children under school age. The big turning point is when your youngest child turns four. By that age, all your children are out of nappies, sleeping through the night and going to school or preschool. Virtually overnight you suddenly have more time for yourself. And the time you spend with your children is better, too. It's taken up less with the tedious, labour-intensive basics – cleaning, changing, feeding, supervising – and more with the delightful two-way interaction that makes family life so fulfilling. As your children become more independent, you'll notice that your own 'self' starts returning, stronger and wiser than before.

2 **Commit to staying together until your oldest child turns five** Don't make any life-changing decisions before then. The first five years of parenting are by far the most difficult – both mothers and fathers can suffer post-natal depression and heightened anxiety levels – and it's no mystery why many couples split up during this time. But if you bail out too early, you could well regret it later when life becomes more manageable. It takes a good five years

to adjust to your new life as parents. Only then, when you're in a more relaxed and rational frame of mind, are you able to see your situation more clearly and by then, many of the problems have resolved themselves. (Obviously this does not apply to relationships where there are issues of infidelity, gambling, addiction or abuse, in which case an early exit is often the best solution.) I'll never forget a conversation I had with a senior TV executive – a single mother of two – at a function. She told me her biggest regret was the break-up of her marriage when the children were aged three and one. 'We're both good people and fundamentally we were really well suited,' she said. 'But when the kids were little, it was so stressful, it's like we both went a bit insane. We weren't ourselves. And by the time we were ourselves again, it was too late – we were divorced.'

3   **Accept your limitations and imperfections** Being the perfect employee, the perfect parent, the perfect spouse and having the perfect home is logistically impossible. In fact, it's so ridiculous you have to wonder why we knock ourselves out trying to achieve it. Congratulate yourself simply for making it through each day. The pay-off is that you'll come out of it caring a lot less about things that don't really matter – like whether you've been wearing your top inside-out and back-to-front all day. If you've been a slave to fashion and other people's opinions all your life, this is truly liberating.

4   **Don't read glossy women's magazines** The trashy ones are just plain nasty about women – in their eyes, we're all either perfect skinny successes, or fat failures – and they'll make you feel bad about yourself no matter what. Even the better quality women's magazines paint an unrealistic picture with their endless stories of 'baby joy' and married bliss. Here's the truth: all of them airbrush

photos. All of them provide clothes, stylists and make-up artists so their interview subjects look perfect. (I know, I've been there. I once had several kilos photoshopped off my arms and back for a glamorous *Madison* photo shoot. I was seven months pregnant but looked like a starving ballerina.)

If you must read magazines at this vulnerable stage of your life, do so with your eyes wide open: they do not reflect reality. As for fashion mags, avoid them at all costs when you are struggling with the work/family juggle. They encourage you to feel dissatisfied with your life and to hanker after stupidly priced designer goods that no normal person can possibly afford. And again, don't believe a word of them. It is simply not possible for the average woman to have a wardrobe full of designer labels, Manolo Blahniks and $1200 handbags. Most of the women featured in fashion magazines either get those things for free because they're in the business, or they're married to wealthy men. Do not compare yourself to them. They're not real.

4 **Be patient and persistent** This is the best way to achieve a fair division of domestic tasks. It is better for everybody – mum, dad and kids – for each individual member of the family to take some responsibility for running the household. Women need to realise that many men do not have the basic skills required for housework, are embarrassed to ask for help, and feel demeaned by the whole idea. There's no point getting angry or putting pressure on them; this only escalates the problem. Start with simple tasks, be positive and appreciative and resist the urge to criticise or take over. Accept that domestic work is never as simple as a 50/50 split, and that people are better at different things. Above all, give credit where it's due. If your spouse is the type of person who'd willingly chase off an intruder, or get up on the roof during a cyclone and

attach a tarpaulin, that's worth quite a few dishwashing credits. They may not have to do it very often – but when they do, it's worth it.

5 **Realise you're not alone** Everyone does it tough when they're juggling work and kids. Everyone. It's easy to look around and think other people are managing so much better than you are. Trust me, they're not. Everybody struggles and everybody puts on a brave face. The most supportive thing you can do for yourself, and others, is to swallow your pride and stop pretending you're perfect. When you allow yourself to be vulnerable, you'll be amazed at the response. People love to help; it makes them feel good about themselves. You just have to reach out to them.

The Big Question

Yep, this is the one that we all want the answer to, the one that keeps us awake after the 3 am feed, the one we really, really beat ourselves up over: is it possible to 'have it all'?

Here's my opinion, as a battle-scarred veteran. Yes, it *is* possible to have it all – just not all at the same time.

If you try to have it all, all at the same time, you'll pay a high price. For some people it's their physical health, or their mental health; for others, the price they pay is their marriage and their family.

Even the scaled-down version of having it all, the one that involves compromises, carries risks and dangers; you need to be aware of them, and learn how to manage them. But for those who want it, and those who have the courage to attempt it, the quest to have it all can be an exhilarating adventure: a life fully lived.

Whether you think it's worth the price – well, that's your decision, and yours alone. I wish you the best of luck in reaching it.

now ...

WE SOLD OUR BIG HOUSE with the big mortgage and moved to a small house in the suburbs. The forced downshift turned out to be a blessing in disguise. Overnight, my commuting time was cut from 10 hours a week to two, and the mortgage was halved. We discovered the luxury of having one bathroom to clean instead of three. In our quest for a simpler, healthier lifestyle, we also got rid of the microwave, the dishwasher, cable TV, the fax, the phone and the answering machine. The tumble drier went into semi-retirement as I rediscovered the old-fashioned pleasure of pegging out clothes in the sunlight. Mario's next creative project is building a vegetable garden, so we can grow at least some of what we eat.

Marcus and Mischa now attend the local primary school. Looking back, those indescribably difficult first five years of parenting has passed in a flash, although at the time it seemed to last forever. The children are no longer my babies, but independent little people with strong opinions, one of which is that grown-ups spend too much time working and not enough playing. With that in mind, I negotiated a

more family-friendly roster, 'buying' more holiday time by taking a cut in salary. I am privileged to work for one of the few employers in Australia which would consider this option.

Through all these changes, the pressure cooker has been my steadfast companion in the kitchen. Now a reliable old friend, it's seen me through every season of my children's lives and quite a few stages of my own. I've introduced numerous friends and acquaintances to the miracle of pressure cooking, and I'm thrilled to read that it's having a renaissance across Australia. I still use it at least twice a week – and I still get a buzz every time I open the lid.

As modern life hurtles on around us, we, like many others, are discovering the joys of a slower pace. The events of the past few years – marriage, parenthood, family health crises, the economic meltdown – have proved that, just like the old days, there are only a few things that really matter. Time – together, and for yourself. Food – grown and shared. Home. Family. And most of all, life. Every precious day of it.

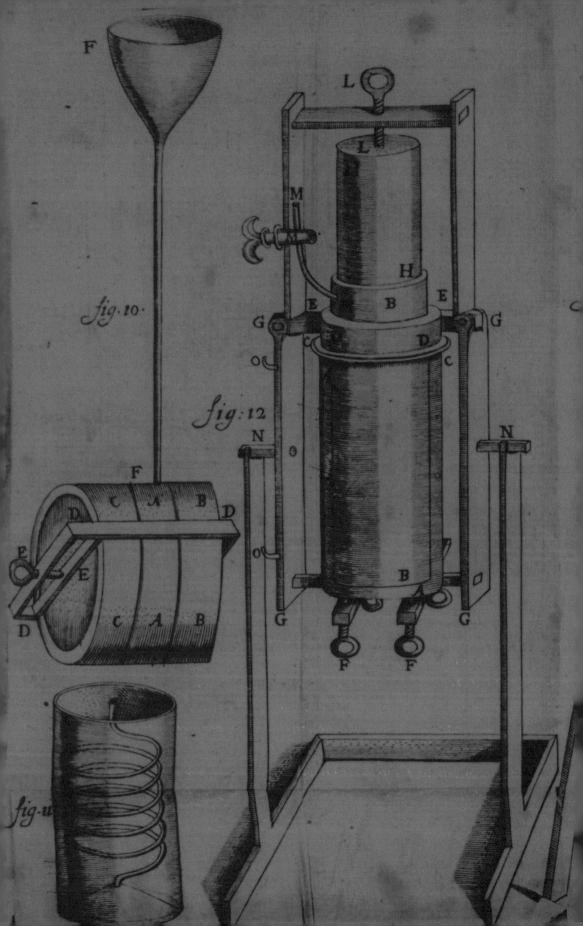

fig: 10.

fig: 12.

fig: 11.

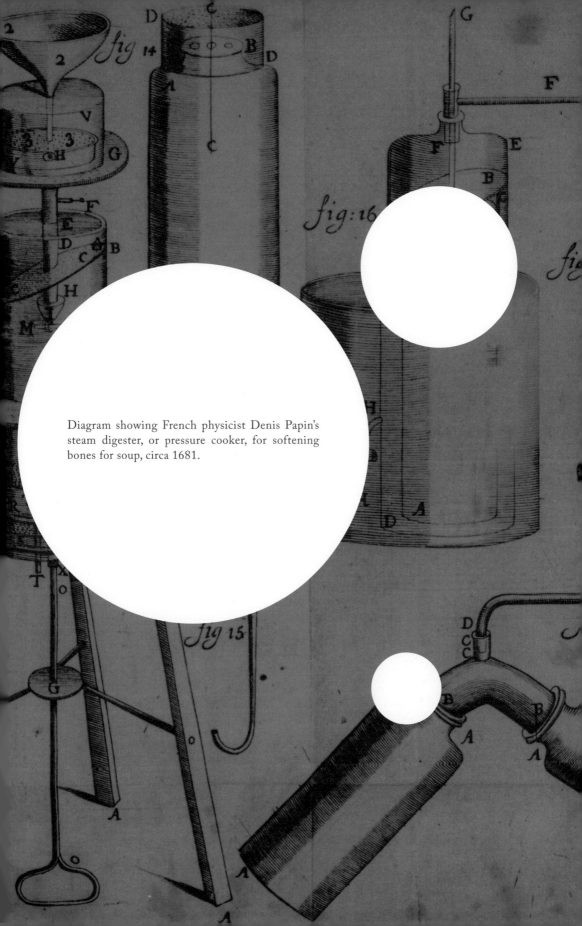

Diagram showing French physicist Denis Papin's steam digester, or pressure cooker, for softening bones for soup, circa 1681.

the Hawkins-Universal makes cooking an easy and delightful task, not only for working mothers and busy housewives, but for bachelors and husbands with culinary pretensions as well!

Old pressure cooker instruction manual [55]

pressure cooking

Only the pressure cooker has the perfect qualities for today's busy, complicated lifestyles. It's fast. It's clean. It's healthy. It's cheap. It's easy. It's environmentally friendly. With everyone going green and frugal, the pressure cooker's time has come.

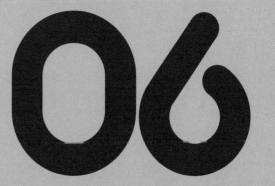

pressure cooking

WHEN I STARTED USING my vintage $5 pressure cooker, I was so excited by the results I could barely sleep. (Stay with me, okay? I don't get out a lot since I had kids!) To me, it seemed like a miracle. I'd spent years slaving over a hot stove using conventional methods and here was a simple, old-fashioned pot that allowed me to make the same meals in a fraction of the time.

Pressure Cooker FAQs

Many of my colleagues are working mothers, and they were fascinated to hear about my pressure cooker.

'I didn't know you could get them any more!' was usually the first response – followed by a lot of questions. Here are the most common.

Why a pressure cooker?
- It saves time. With a pressure cooker, you can prepare healthy family meals, in bulk, in a third of the time, or even less. Meals that normally

take hours are ready in minutes. A one-hour soup is cooked in 20 minutes. Risotto – which usually requires an hour of patient stirring – is done to perfection in 7 minutes. And because all the cooking takes place beneath a locked lid, without any supervision or intervention on your part, it frees you up to do something else during that time, such as putting on a load of washing (a good example of time squeezing).

- It saves energy. A pressure cooker reduces cooking time by up to 70 per cent, which means up to 70 per cent less gas or electricity is needed to power it. In many parts of the world, there's a pressure cooker in almost every kitchen for that reason.

- It saves money. As well as using a fraction of the energy, a pressure cooker allows you to cook in bulk and freeze excess portions for later use. It also tenderises tougher (and usually cheaper) cuts of meat, allowing you to save on your grocery bill.

  Here's an example of how much money you can save. At the supermarket, a single portion of fresh, vacuum-packed soup sells for around $6 to $7. For the same money, you can buy the ingredients to make enough soup for 10 servings. My local deli sells single serves of homemade beef curry for $10. I can make five times as much in my pressure cooker for the same price.

- It saves on cleaning up. A pressure cooker is the perfect one-pot meal, which reduces the amount of washing up you have to do afterwards. Also, because pressure cooking relies on steaming, there's no scrubbing or scouring involved in cleaning the cooker – you can usually just rinse it out with water.

- It's healthier and cleaner. High-speed pressure cooking locks in nutrients and, as a bonus, wipes out bacteria. (Hospitals use a type of pressure cooker, an autoclave, to sterilise medical instruments.) And because the lid is locked on airtight, you don't get any nasty cooking smells or grease splatters in your kitchen.

Do they still make pressure cookers these days?

Yes, they do. These days, pressure cookers are miracles of modern engineering – made of stainless steel with all sorts of bells and whistles – but they still work on the same principle. There's a huge range available, in various sizes and ranging in price from $49 to more than $500. (I paid $79 for my 8-litre, stainless-steel, Spanish cooker at a discount supermarket.)

Pressure cookers went out of fashion in Australia a few decades ago, but they've always been around and are still popular in many parts of the world. My 82-year-old mother still uses her old aluminium Hawkins – it's more than 60 years old, and too pitted for direct-contact cooking, but it's great for steaming her golden syrup puddings [see page 249 for the recipe].

Don't they explode?

No, not these days. The myth of the exploding pressure cooker has been blown way out of proportion. The early pressure cookers were mass-produced just after World War II to satisfy a huge pent-up demand for them. The design and materials were inferior to those of today, and there are numerous accounts of these first-generation cookers blowing their tops, in most cases resulting in a messy stove or, at worst, dinner splattered on the ceiling.

Unfortunately, the old horror stories gave pressure cookers an undeserved reputation as ticking time bombs, which has persisted for decades, despite all the technological advances. Interestingly, the term 'pressure cooker' as a synonym for an explosive or dangerous situation first appeared in *The Spectator* magazine in 1958, no doubt as a result of these stories.[56]

But I'm still scared to use one!

Don't be. Modern pressure cookers have so many safety features even a complete idiot can use one. Even if – worst-case scenario – you left the pressure cooker on high heat and went out shopping, the safety valve would kick in and release the pressure at a constant rate (rather than the volcanic eruptions of the old models). There is no way the lid is going to fly off. The other thing that modern design has eliminated is the scary hissing and jiggling noises that used to be an indicator of rising pressure. Today's pressure cookers are quiet and safe, and once you've used one a couple of times, you'll wonder how you ever did without it.

How does a pressure cooker work? Isn't it the same as steaming?

Kind of. It's like steaming on steroids! A pressure cooker is basically a large, heavy pot with a lid that locks on and seals airtight with a rubber gasket. Ingredients are placed in it, along with a small amount of water. When heated, steam builds up inside and has nowhere to escape, so the temperature and the pressure start to rise. Under full pressure, the food inside is being cooked at a very high temperature (around 122°C as opposed to normal boiling point of 100°C). This cuts the cooking time by up to two-thirds. The pressure is controlled by reducing the heat; a system of vents and valves allows the steam to be released safely should it build up beyond a certain level. Once the cooking period is over, the cooker is removed from the heat. As it cools, the pressure drops, allowing the lid to be removed safely.

What sort of meals can you make in a pressure cooker?

A pressure cooker is an extremely versatile appliance that can be used to cook a variety of meat, poultry, vegetable, rice, pasta and sweet dishes, very quickly. Examples of pressure cooker meals include beef curry, roast chicken, minestrone soup, pork spare ribs, garlic prawns and chocolate pudding. With the lid off, it can be used just as any other regular pot or pan, to brown and sauté food. With the lid on, its primary purpose is high-pressure steaming. For that reason, it is most commonly used to make soups, stews, casseroles and curries. However, it is also a quick way to roast meat (by browning it first in an open cooker before closing and cooking at high pressure). Using racks and separators, it is also possible to cook a number of things at the same time.

Is there anything you can't cook in a pressure cooker?

The main benefit of a pressure cooker is to save time, so there's little point using it for food which already has a short cooking time, such as some vegetables and fish. The one thing you must never do is 'pressure fry'. While it's okay to fry food in a pressure cooker with the lid off, once the lid goes on there must be a minimum amount of water inside to allow the pressure cooker to work safely. Boiling oil under pressure is extremely dangerous, and you should never use more than a quarter of a cup of oil in any recipe, regardless of how much other liquid is in it.

Why not just use a microwave? They're fast ...

Ugh! Don't get me started on microwaves. For starters, they heat food unevenly. If you put something in a microwave to defrost it'll come out completely cooked in some parts and raw and frozen in others. Second, they're a nightmare to clean if you get food spattered on the

172

inside. Third, in my job I hear an awful lot about delinquent youths amusing themselves by putting small animals into microwaves, and that makes me uneasy every time I look at one.

But most of all, I just hate the idea of cooking food by putting it inside a white metal box and blasting it with microwaves. I don't even know what these waves are, or how they work – do you? Don't get me wrong, I'm not bagging microwave ovens completely. They're great for heating up leftovers and baby bottles. But I find the idea of making an entire meal in one very unappealing. Give me an old-fashioned pot, some water and a natural heat source any day.

Well ... What about slow cookers? Aren't they good for busy people?

In theory, slow cookers sound like a good idea, and I considered them carefully before seeing the light and buying a pressure cooker instead. The main drawback with a slow cooker is that it's very, um, slow. The way they work is: you put all your ingredients in the cooker in the morning, then by the time you come home from work, your meal is ready. That's fine if you work nine to five, and your mornings are relatively calm and ordered.

If, however, you have multiple family members milling around demanding breakfast, sympathy, packed lunches, matching shoes and lifts to different schools while you're trying to get ready for work, the last thing you have time to do is prepare the evening meal. With a slow cooker, you need to be there in the morning to turn it on, and in the evening to turn it off. You also need to have all your ingredients on hand first thing in the morning.

The pressure cooker is simply more flexible and convenient. It allows you to make a complete meal in a 20-minute window of time, whenever one becomes available. So in short: slow cookers work well for some people. But personally, I think they're not that convenient for busy people whose routine is frequently disrupted by one domestic crisis or another. And I'll also admit: I'm just not that keen on the idea of my food being on a very low heat for a very long period of time. Makes me think of bains marie in dodgy restaurants.

Is it okay to use mum's old cooker, or do I need to buy a new one?
Vintage pressure cookers are fun to use because of their retro styling and nostalgia value. If, like me, you enjoy channelling your inner 1950s housewife, the old hissing, jiggle-top cookers have a charm and personality you just can't beat. But it's important all the parts are in good condition and you use them carefully. Manufacturers still stock replacement parts for many old cookers (check the website www. pressurecooker.com.au).

I love using my old Hawkins, and it works perfectly, but like most vintage cookers, it's only small. Once I was hooked on pressure cooking I invested in a new, bigger, stainless-steel cooker suitable for bulk cooking. The advantage of new cookers, apart from the bigger sizes available, is that they're made using the latest technology and design and they have all sorts of safety features.

What size should I get?
The old pressure cookers are generally around 6 litres in size, which is fine for single meals but not so good for cooking in bulk. I have an 8 litre pressure cooker and for a family of four, I find that's big enough. It allows me to cook enough to last 2 or 3 meals, but it's still small enough to use easily, if I just want to cook up a quick single portion of something. If you've got a bigger family, the new pressure cookers also come in 10, 12 and 14 litre sizes.

Where can I get one?

Specialty homewares shops have a good range of the most popular cookers and they also have websites where you can compare prices and features. You may also find pressure cookers at your local large retailer or department store – but call ahead to make sure they have them. I picked up mine at a discount supermarket that had a one-off delivery of them. Spend an hour or two on the internet researching the different types of cookers to see which one suits you best in terms of size, features and price. I'd suggest the following websites: underpressure.com.au, pressurecooker.com.au, petersofkensington.com.au and victoriasbasement.com.au.

1

Napoleon Bonaparte played a part in it. In the 18th century, he offered a reward to anyone who could invent a way of preserving food for his army, leading to the development of pressure canning – the forerunner of pressure cooking.

2

The famous food writer Margaret Fulton helped introduce the pressure cooker to Australia. One of her first jobs was selling them to department stores and retailers after World War II.

five things you didn't know about pressure cooking

3

Colonel Sanders stumbled across pressure cooking in the late 1930s, and adapted it to speed up the cooking time of one of the original 'fast foods' – Kentucky Fried Chicken.

4

The first Australian pressure cookers were made by the Commonwealth Aircraft Corporation, using melted-down saucepans originally donated to make warplanes.

5

In 2005, Cuba's President Fidel Castro announced plans to distribute millions of subsidised pressure cookers to reduce energy consumption and boost the economy.

The Pressure Cooker Story

It all starts nearly 400 years ago, when the French physicist Denys Papin makes a cast-iron pot with a lock-on lid and a safety valve and calls it a 'steam digester'. He takes it to London to demonstrate it, showing that when the lid of his primitive pressure cooker is locked on, 'food cooks rapidly, requiring less fuel, and that even old meat becomes tender ...'[57]

It takes a few centuries for scientists and manufacturers to figure out how to regulate pressure, and more importantly, make vessels that don't explode. But the basic principle is a winner and in the late 1700s it is used to develop the canning process in which food is vacuum-sealed under pressure. Napoleon Bonaparte seizes on the idea to feed his massive army. (Unfortunately nobody thinks to invent a can opener at the same time, so they have to use bayonets.)

In the days before refrigeration, pressure canning means that food can be kept for long periods of time without going off. While tinned food is invented for military purposes – the troops at Waterloo are among the first to get their rations in cans – it doesn't take long for business to realise its commercial potential and take it to the United States to make some serious money.

The early American pressure canners are enormous vessels designed for large-scale industrial use, but by the early 1900s, housewives are starting to demand smaller versions for the home. The term 'pressure cooker' first appears in print in 1915 in *The Journal of Home Economics*, and, in 1919, the women's magazine *The Delineator* reports: 'Of all modern household devices on the market today, there is no one article which does more towards lessening household burdens than the pressure cooker.'[58] Over the next 20 years the design evolves as housewives begin using the cooker for much more than just a canning device.

In 1939, the Presto company unveils the first modern-style pressure cooker at New York's World Fair. The new, saucepan-style design is an instant success and is soon being mass-produced by factories across Europe and the United States.

The Australian Love Affair with Pressure Cookers

Word quickly reaches Downunder of the miraculous new appliance that dramatically speeds up cooking time. But as soon as overseas factories start churning out pressure cookers, World War II is declared. Production of all kitchenware comes to an abrupt halt as aluminium supplies are diverted for military use – in particular, for building warplanes.

In Australia, the Commonwealth Aircraft Corporation (CAC) appeals to the nation's housewives for help, calling on the women of Australia to donate their aluminium pots and pans to be used to make military aircraft.

'As it happened, the household implements weren't needed, so at the end of the war (CAC chief) John Storey ... was left with a mountain of old saucepans,' the food writer Margaret Fulton will recall in her memoirs many years later. [59] 'What was he to do with them? Pressure cookers seemed to be the answer.' Inspired by the pressure cooker's success in America, Storey decides to use the huge stockpile of scrap aluminium to make an Australian version.

The plan is also a handy way of keeping the Aircraft Corporation's employees busy once the war ends. With military aircraft no longer in big demand, the CAC starts turning out domestic goods and building materials in response to the post-war housing boom. The pressure cooker is one of its biggest sellers. By 1947, it has produced 75 000 of them, enough to make the CAC's foundry almost self-sufficient. [60]

'Your CAC Pressure Cooker has been tested to stand at least double the maximum working pressure, so that it is always absolutely safe,' the instruction booklet promises.

Within a year or two, pressure cooker production is taken over by John Storey's new business venture, the Overseas Corporation, which manufactures and retails a wide range of goods. Of all the company's products, it is the pressure cooker, rebranded as Namco, which becomes its biggest seller. A young Margaret Fulton – who later becomes one of Australia's best-loved cooks and food writers – is employed by Storey as a home economist to teach people how to use the new appliance.

Pressure rises …

The austerity of the war years created a huge pent-up demand for household goods. In particular, thrifty housewives are desperate to get their hands on the new energy-efficient pressure cooker, which allows them to make delicious meals from even the cheapest cuts of meat.

With Australian women clamouring for them, the company needs to get pressure cookers into the market in large numbers. Margaret Fulton is promoted to NSW sales manager, responsible for getting the Namco cookers into department stores and retailers.

'We were selling pressure cookers like hot cakes,' Fulton writes later. 'So well, in fact, that we were soon running out of aluminium.' [61]

Even the Prime Minister, Ben Chifley, is a convert. In 1948, having made inquiries about pressure cookers, Chifley receives one from John Storey. The Prime Minister thanks him for 'this most desirable present for the wife' and insists on paying for it. [62]

But even though the Overseas Corporation is producing 25 000 pressure cookers a month, it still cannot meet Australia's demand.

Imported cookers quickly step in to fill the gap. One of the most popular is the Hawkins, which my father remembers was considered 'more upmarket than a Namco. Everyone had a Namco. Your mother was very specific about wanting a Hawkins when we got married. It was the very latest thing.'

'To the housewives of Australia comes the world's finest pressure cooker!' announces an advertisement in *The Australian Women's Weekly Cookery Book* of 1948. 'America's finest pressure cooker, made by Hawkins of London. The Hawkins is so very safe, so sure and so easy to clean. Anyone can obtain perfect results with a Hawkins.'

For several decades, the pressure cooker is a mainstay of Australian kitchens. From the 1940s through to the '60s, every bride gets a pressure cooker. Generations of children grow up with the familiar hissing sound of the old jiggle-top cooker in the background as Mum cooks the weekly lamb stew, or steams her golden syrup pudding.

Pressure falls ...
But in the 1970s, following a similar trend in the United States, the pressure cooker's star begins to fade. Food fashions change; Australians are embracing different cuisines and cooking methods introduced by immigrants. At the same time, convenience food – frozen and packet meals – is starting to gain a foothold. Technology comes up with new appliances and gadgets. Crockpots – the slow-cooking polar opposite of the pressure cooker – begin popping up on kitchen benchtops like mushrooms. Then the microwave bursts onto the scene, and by the mid-1980s, it looks like the pressure cooker's days are over.

Elsewhere in the world, though, the pressure cooker never goes out of style. In countries where cooking fuel is expensive or in short supply, it continues to be the most important piece of equipment in the kitchen. To this day, it is used daily by millions of people. In India, around 80 per cent of the urban population owns a pressure cooker.

In Cuba, it's considered vital to the domestic economy. And it's not just poorer countries – in many wealthy European nations, pressure cooking is a part of everyday life. In fact, Europe leads the world in the design and manufacture of top-of-the-range pressure cookers, something it took over when the US market lost interest.

And rises again ...

Today, the pressure cooker stands ready to resume its rightful place in the Australian kitchen. Safer and more technologically advanced than ever, there is no single appliance more suited to the frantic pace and tight budgets of our modern world. The microwave, once hailed as the future of cooking, turned out to be just a great way to heat up leftovers. Slow cookers turned out to be just too, well, slow.

Only the pressure cooker has the perfect qualities for today's busy, complicated lifestyles. It's fast. It's clean. It's healthy. It's cheap. It's easy. It's environmentally friendly.

With everyone going green and frugal, the pressure cooker's time has come.

How to Use a Pressure Cooker

There are many brands of pressure cooker, but they all work on the same principle. These are the basic steps for all pressure cookers, both old-fashioned and modern, regardless of their individual differences.
(1) Place ingredients and water into the cooker.
(2) Place over high heat.
(3) Close the lid, and bring to high pressure.
(4) When high pressure is reached, reduce the heat to the lowest possible temperature at which it is possible to maintain high pressure.
(5) Cook at high pressure for a defined period of time.

(6) Remove from heat.

(7) Release the pressure.

(8) Carefully remove the lid.

The key to this type of cooking is reaching high pressure as quickly as possible, maintaining that pressure at a stable level, then releasing the pressure at the speed and time required by the recipe.

What is pressure and how does it work?

If you fill a pot with water and put it on a hot stove, it will start to boil once it reaches 100°C. That's the normal boiling point of water at sea level. But if you seal the pot with a tightly fitting lid, steam starts to build up inside it. Because there is nowhere for the steam to escape, pressure builds inside the pot. As the pressure builds, the temperature rises. Once the pressure reaches 15 psi (pounds per square inch), the temperature is around 122°C – much higher than boiling point. Under these conditions, food cooks very quickly.

Some modern pressure cookers have different pressure settings, so you can cook at low, medium or high pressure. However, the high-pressure setting of 15 psi is the standard for virtually all recipes.

The most crucial step in pressure cooking is number 4 on my list: reducing the heat as soon as the cooker reaches high pressure. Reducing the heat stops the pressure continuing to build and maintains it at a safe level. (If you forget to reduce the heat, as I occasionally do, the pressure cooker will soon let you know about it by spitting steam and hissing! If you do nothing, modern pressure cookers have a safety feature which kicks in to release the steam safely.)

How to tell when the pressure cooker reaches high pressure

With the old-fashioned cookers, you'd know when they reached high pressure because the weight on top of the steam vent would start to jump and jiggle, which is why they were known as jiggle-tops. The modern pressure cookers take the guesswork out of it completely. Most of them have a brightly coloured indicator which pops up when the cooker reaches high pressure and then disappears from view when the pressure drops.

Reducing the heat

Once the pressure indicator pops into view, telling you the cooker has reached high pressure, you need to reduce the heat immediately. This will stop the pressure continuing to build to a level which would trigger the safety mechanism. Knowing just how far to reduce the heat is the only tricky part of the process, and it all depends on the type of stovetop you're using.

All heating elements are different, especially electric ones, which are slower to respond to the temperature controls. You need to lower the heat to a point where it is high enough to maintain the pressure inside the pot, but low enough to keep the pressure stable. Once the cooker has reached high pressure, it does not require a lot of heat to keep it up there, which is why pressure cooking uses so little energy compared with regular methods. So how low is low enough to maintain pressure at a stable level? On my old electric stove, it was around the one-third (or 4 o'clock) mark on the temperature control knob, and even lower for longer recipes. On my new gas stove, I take it down to the halfway mark. After using your pressure cooker once or twice, you'll quickly get to know how far to turn the temperature down on your particular stovetop.

Don't be worried about getting it wrong. If you don't turn it down enough, the pressure cooker will start to hiss, prompting you to reduce the heat even further. (If you're alarmed by the hissing, you can just take it off the heat altogether until it cools down a bit.) And if you turn it down too low, the worst that can happen is that you lose pressure, and the food is undercooked. If that happens, just stick it back on the heat, bring it to high pressure again and give it another go!

Please note: in the recipe section of this book, I use the term 'lower the heat' to mean 'lower the heat to the point at which high pressure is maintained and stabilised'.

Setting the timer

A timer is an essential part of pressure cooking, for two reasons. First, the alarm reminds you to take the pressure cooker off the stove-top, just in case you've forgotten about it. Second, it means your cooking times will be accurate to the last second. Because pressure cooking times are so short, even a minute or two can make a big difference to the result. For that reason, it's really important to follow the cooking times given in the recipes, and the only way you can do that accurately is to use a timer.

You can pick up cheap timers in the cookware aisle of supermarkets. Ideally, use an electronic one – they're more accurate than the wind-up variety. If possible, buy one that you can attach to your belt or carry in your pocket. That way, if you're distracted away from the kitchen while the pressure cooker is on, the timer's beeping will remind you to go back and take it off the stove. **Note: timing starts the moment you reduce the heat to stabilise the pressure.**

Reducing pressure

Once your timer goes off, you'll know that your food has been cooking at high pressure for the required length of time. The next step is to take the cooker off the heat and reduce the pressure so you can remove the lid. There are three ways of reducing pressure. The technique you use will depend on whether the recipe requires the pressure to be released quickly or slowly.

184

1 **Natural release.** This is the easiest, the slowest and the most common way to depressurise a cooker. You simply take it off the heat, and let it cool naturally. As the temperature falls, the pressure comes down and eventually (in about 10 minutes), the pressure indicator will drop away. At this point, you are able to remove the lid of the cooker. As a precaution, you should always remove the lid carefully, even when the pressure has dropped. The natural release method is used for meals that benefit from a bit of resting time, such as stews and soups – it's the least amount of bother for the cook.

2 **Cold water release.** This method is used for food which has a short cooking time, such as green vegetables, rice or fish. It is the fastest way to reduce the temperature inside the cooker, which in turn depressurises the cooker. While the food is cooking, run about 10 cm of cold water into the sink. When the timer goes off, carry the cooker carefully to the sink and sit it in the cold water. To speed up the drop in temperature, you can also turn the tap on and gently run cold water down the side of the cooker, and over a little of the top. But be very careful NOT to run the water over the vent or the valve section, as it will interfere with the depressurising process and could damage the lid.

3 **Quick release.** The old cookers only had the first two methods of depressurising, but the modern cookers all have a mechanism that releases pressure quickly. On my cooker, you turn the pressure regulating valve to the 'steam release' setting. Steam comes out in a controlled flow, taking the pressure down with it. It's not as fast as the cold water release and it does make your kitchen quite steamy. But because it reduces pressure without reducing the temperature of the food, it's great for those recipes where you need to interrupt the cooking process to add more ingredients.

Once you've done that, you can then replace the lid and return the cooker to high pressure very quickly to continue cooking. I also use the quick release knob if the water method is taking too long and I'm impatient to see the results of my cooking!

THE SAFE COOK does not use the quick-release method with foods that are mostly liquid, such as soup, or food that tends to foam and expand under pressure, like beans and pasta.

Gas vs electric

It doesn't matter whether you have a gas stove or an electric one. Pressure cookers work well on any heat source – which is why they're also perfect for camping or boating, because you can use them with small portable stoves. Temperature is certainly easier to control on a gas stove, and it's my personal preference because it responds faster.

Until recently, it was my luck in life to inherit an electric stove wherever I lived. I came to know and tolerate them over the years, and I've never had any problems pressure cooking on an electric element. Some cooks like to have two electric elements going when they pressure cook – one on high heat, the other on low – so that when the cooker reaches high pressure, they can switch it over to low heat immediately. I tried that once or twice, but personally, I found it wasn't worth the hassle.

The other important thing is that no matter what kind of element you use, it should be slightly smaller than the base of the pressure cooker. Never use an element that is too big for the cooker. If using a gas cooker, the flame should never go up the side of the cooker.

If you have an induction stove which works on magnetism, double-check with the manufacturer that it is safe to use your stainless-steel pressure cooker on it. (Induction stovetops will not work with older pressure cookers, which are made on non-magnetic aluminium.)

Fill 'er up!

The general rule is that a pressure cooker should be no more than two-thirds full (including water). However, there are some foods that expand under pressure, including rice, pasta, dried beans and lentils. When using those ingredients, only fill the cooker up to the halfway point and bring them to pressure over medium heat. It is also a good idea to keep soup to the halfway point as well.

All these foods should be depressurised slowly, by the natural method, and extra care taken when removing the lid.

Safety Checklist

- Always read the instruction manual for your pressure cooker thoroughly. Become familiar with the various parts of it, what they are called and what they are used for. Lock and unlock the lid several times before you start cooking so it becomes second nature. (If you have lost your instruction booklet, contact the manufacturer for a replacement. If you have a vintage pressure cooker without a manual, keep an eye on eBay and other auction sites, which often list them. The national and state libraries also have a good selection of old pressure cooker manuals.)
- Every time you use the cooker, check that the vents and valves are clear, and that the rubber gasket is in good condition. Make sure the pop-up pressure indicator moves freely. If using an old pressure cooker, look through the vent pipe to see if it's clear – it's only tiny, but you should be able to see daylight through it.
- Always use a timer. As well as ensuring your food is cooked for exactly the right amount of time, it also beeps to remind you to take the cooker off the stove. If there's a lot happening around you, sometimes that important step can be overlooked!

- Always follow the recipe, paying close attention to the cooking time, the amount of liquid required, and the method of release. Read the recipe from beginning to end before starting it, so you are not caught by surprise at any point.
- Always remember to turn the heat down as soon as the cooker reaches high pressure. This is very easy to forget. (Well, easy for me. I seem to be an expert at it!)
- Don't leave the pressure cooker unattended. If you have young children, make sure they stay away from it, and keep the kitchen floor clear of toys so you don't trip while moving the pressure cooker from the stove to the benchtop.
- Before using your pressure cooker, give it a test-run by boiling two cups of water in it. When the water boils, lock on the lid, bring it to high pressure, then release the pressure naturally. Then do it again, using the cold water release method. This will get you used to how the pressure cooker works, so that you're relaxed and confident when you make your first meal in it.
- The pressure cooker should never be more than two-thirds full. With soup and foods that expand or foam under pressure, it should only be filled to the halfway point.
- Always use a minimum amount of water – check the instruction booklet for the recommended amount for your cooker. It is generally about 1 cup (250 ml). However, be careful not to use too much water, as that may affect the result. Stick to the recipe.
- Never use more than quarter of a cup of oil in any recipe, and NEVER attempt to 'pressure fry' food. It's extremely dangerous. Every recipe must contain water.

Advanced Pressure Cooking

This book only deals with basic pressure cooking and preparing simple meals in the quickest time possible. But if you really love pressure cooking, and you want to take it to the next level, it is capable of much more complex recipes, using a number of techniques.

For example, you can cook a number of different foods in a pressure cooker by interrupting the process and adding different ingredients at different times. This requires depressurising the cooker (usually by the quick method), then repressurising it.

You can also cook a number of different elements in a meal at the same time, by using pans or steamer baskets that stack on top of each other. A simple example of this would be cooking a curry in the bottom of the cooker, and using a rack with a bowl on top to cook the rice at the same time, and on top of that, you could rest a steamer with some vegies inside. You can even make bread and cakes in a pressure cooker. The possibilities are limited only by your enthusiasm.

Learn From My Mistakes

During the 18 months I've been pressure cooking, I've experienced most of the common problems encountered by novice users. Sometimes the mistake is obvious and easy to fix. At other times I've had to do recipes over and over again to figure out where I'm going wrong. Here are some of my mistakes and how I've corrected them.

The problem: Food burning and sticking to the bottom of the cooker. This was the bane of my life, and I spent many hours scrubbing my cooker with steel wool before I sorted it out. I found that meat dishes in particular (and to a lesser extent, anything with peas or lentils in it) would end up leaving a thick, scorched, black mess on the bottom of the cooker that was difficult to get off. The food itself would also taste burned, which meant I had to throw it out.

The causes: Through trial and error, I discovered I was making four basic errors. The first (and most important) error was adding too much liquid. Today's modern pressure cookers need very little water to work efficiently, and adding too much made it difficult for the cooker to produce enough steam to come to pressure. While it boiled and bubbled away on high heat, trying vainly to reach high pressure, the food would burn.

The second mistake I made was mixing tomato products (like tomato paste and crushed tomatoes) in with the other ingredients. According to my bible, *Miss Vickie's Big Book of Pressure Cooker Recipes*, tomato products have a high sugar content and are prone to burning if they touch the bottom of the cooker at high heat.

The third mistake I made was to let heavy pulses like lentils and dried peas drift to the bottom of the cooker while it was heating up, with the result that they often got stuck there and burned.

The fourth mistake was dusting meat with flour before browning it when making stews and casseroles. Here I am in disagreement with my goddess, Miss Vickie, who recommends the use of flour in this way, both as a thickening agent, and because the crusty brown bits it forms add flavour. In my experience, every time I dusted meat with flour, it ended up scorching the bottom of the cooker.

The solutions: Use only a minimum amount of liquid, as per the recipe and the manufacturer's instructions.

Place tomato paste and tinned tomatoes gently on top of the other ingredients, as the last thing you do just before locking the lid shut. When cooking lentils and dried peas, bring the rest of the soup to boiling point first. Add the lentils or dried peas last, and give them a quick stir before locking the lid shut.

When browning meat, do not coat with flour first. With thick stews and sauces, bring them to boiling point while stirring constantly, before locking the lid on. The cooker should then reach high pressure very quickly, and you'll be able to reduce the heat sooner, before the food burns.

The problem: Cooker takes ages to come to pressure. It usually takes a couple of minutes to reach high pressure, but on several occasions, I have waited up to 15 minutes and almost given up.

The cause: Again, using too much liquid. This is just as bad as using too little. Today's cookers are designed to use very little liquid, and adding too much means the cooker can't produce enough steam to come to pressure. Instead, it boils away interminably and often burns the food in the process.

A cooker may also take a long time to come to pressure when it's filled to capacity. More food takes longer to heat, and until the temperature rises to a certain point, the pressure will not start to rise. When I use a large amount of crisp, cold vegetables in a recipe (for example in the Summer Vegetable Compote), I notice that it always takes a long time to come to pressure, sometimes up to 15 minutes. The reason is that cold vegetables simply take longer to heat up.

The solution: Check the recipe and use less liquid (but never less than the minimum amount recommended by the manufacturer, usually around 1 cup or 250ml).

The problem: Soggy vegetables.

The cause: Overcooking.

The solution: Following the cooking times recommended in your cooker's manual. If it's not detailed enough, go to the website missvickie.com, which has a comprehensive guide to cooking times.

The problem: Hard vegetables.

The cause: Undercooking, or not cutting them into small enough pieces.

The solution: Adjust the size of the pieces and follow the cooking times recommended in your cooker's manual. If it's not detailed enough, the website missvickie.com has a comprehensive guide to cooking times.

The problem: A small amount of steam, hissing and drops of water coming out of the lid before the cooker reaches high pressure.

The cause: It's normal for a small amount of steam and a few drops of water to leak out as the cooker heats up and expels the air inside it. That should stop as soon as pressure is reached. You may also hear a faint hissing or whistling sound as the cooker approaches high pressure, then a sudden silence when the valve closes off. Again, that is normal.

The solution: If there's an excessive amount of steam and hissing, which continues even when the cooker has reached pressure, check the valve – it may need cleaning or replacing. And if the hissing and steam starts AFTER you've reached high pressure, then you haven't turned the heat down enough.

The problem: Sauces are too liquid, even when the correct amount of water is used.

The cause: Some dishes need to be thickened after pressure cooking, just as they do in regular cooking.

The solution: There are several easy ways to thicken a sauce, stew or casserole. The time to do this is at the end of the pressure cooking process, not the beginning. The first way is to make a thick paste of butter and flour (similar to the way you start a white sauce). Heat it in a saucepan, then stir it into the cooked meal once the pressure cooker

192

lid comes off. Return it to the heat, with the lid off, and stir until the mixture thickens. The second way is to make a paste of cornflour and water, and add it in the same way. And the cheat's way to soak up excess liquid is to add a few tablespoons of couscous once the lid comes off, while it's still hot.

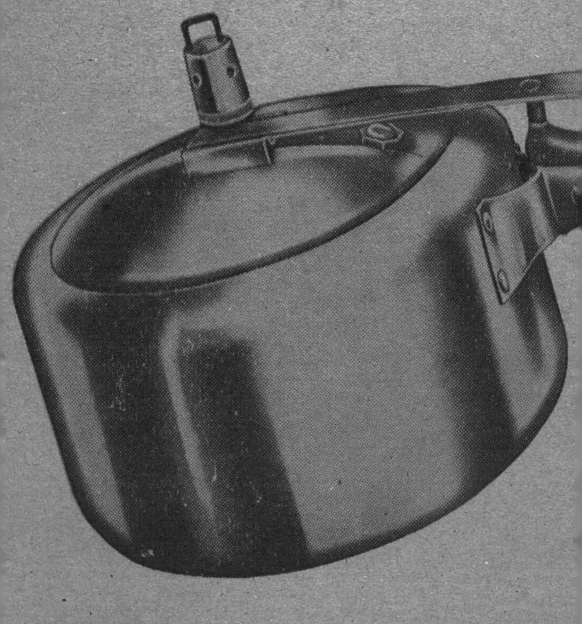

7 big features of the *Hawkins* PRESSURE COOKER

to make dry
toast properly,
a great deal of
attention is
required; much
more than
most people
suppose.

Mrs Beeton's Book of Household Management, 1861

recipes

Only the pressure cooker has the perfect qualities for today's busy, complicated lifestyles. It's fast. It's clean. It's healthy. It's cheap. It's easy. It's environmentally friendly. With everyone going green and frugal, the pressure cooker's time has come.

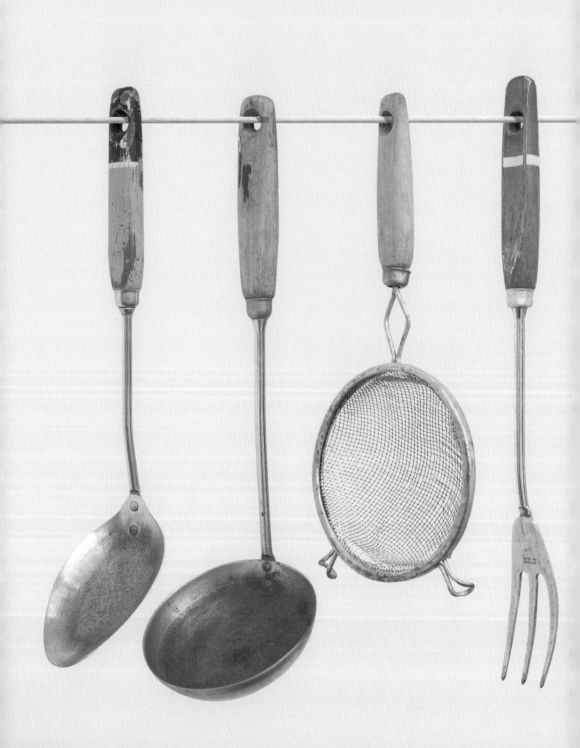

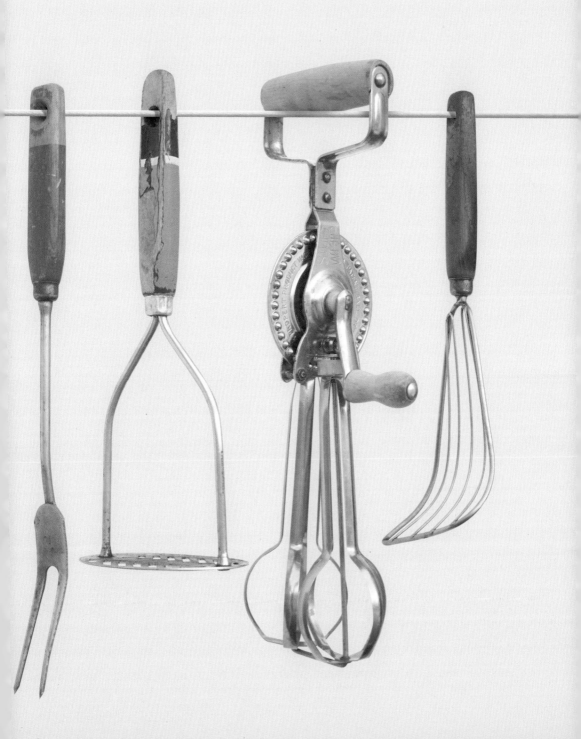

recipes

SO, HERE COMES THE FUN PART – actually cooking something! If you're new to pressure cooking, don't be nervous. Pressure cooking is remarkably easy – easier than cooking dry toast, in fact. When you've done it once or twice, you'll be surprised at how quickly you become proficient at it. Not that you'll ever get bored by it. I've made hundreds of meals in my cooker, and I still get that little thrill of anticipation before I take the lid off and see how it's turned out – a bit like opening a Christmas present.

The main difference you'll find with pressure cooking is how quick it is. With most regular cooking methods, preparation time is the shortest part of the process. With pressure cooking, it's the longest. It takes you more time to get the ingredients together than to actually cook them.

The recipes in this section are personal favourites that I make regularly for my family. Most of them use the pressure cooker, but I've included a few that use the regular cooking method – I've included both because they're all part of my 'survival cooking' repertoire.

Regardless of cooking method, all of them are suitable to make in bulk and freeze.

It's only a small selection, and there are thousands more pressure-cooker recipes out there for you to try if you're feeling adventurous. These are the ones that work for me – they're basic, easy and they suit the demands of a full-time job and a boisterous young family. Hopefully, once you've tried pressure cooking, you'll be inspired to carry on with it, and adapt your own favourite recipes to it.

As I've explained earlier, this book is not intended to be a comprehensive guide to pressure cooking. It's an introduction only. While all pressure cookers operate on the same basic principle, there are individual differences depending on the style and brand. So before you start cooking, please read the manufacturer's instructions for your cooker thoroughly, paying close attention to the safety guidelines.

Okay, now that I've covered myself – let's get cooking!

Please note: in these recipes, the term 'reduce heat' means 'reduce heat to the point at which high pressure is maintained and stabilised'.

First Things First: Stock

Stock is the rich, tasty liquid that adds flavour to soups, casseroles and other dishes. In the old days, making stock used to be one of the cook's most time-consuming tasks, but with a pressure cooker, it becomes ridiculously easy. Instead of taking two hours, it takes 20 minutes.

I know what you're thinking: what a hassle! I can just buy stock, that's even quicker!

You're right, it IS quicker to buy processed stock. I usually have a couple of those small tetra-pack containers of liquid stock in my pantry for emergencies. But the reason I recommend making your own is that it tastes so much better and it's SO much healthier (especially if you're cooking for a baby – the processed stuff is packed with salt and you shouldn't give it to them).

Homemade stock is also a great way to use up your vegetable off-cuts, chicken carcasses, leftover herbs and all the other bits and pieces that would otherwise go to waste. (It's called frugality and thanks to the Global Financial Crisis, we're all becoming a lot better at it.)

Making your own stock in bulk then freezing it in different-sized portions also means you've always got exactly the right amount on hand. And it's very, very quick and easy. If I can make a good stock, anyone can.

A couple of things to remember:

- Stock is made from bones, as opposed to just meat, and has a jelly-like consistency when it cools. Don't be put off by the look of it – it's just the result of the proteins and the gelatine in the bones, which is all good stuff.
- Broth is made using meat only (for example, a couple of chicken thighs or breasts). It is clearer and has a more delicate flavour. I tend to make broth more than stock, only because I don't always have chicken bones handy.
- Freezing stock and broth in portions is a convenient way to have just the right amount at your fingertips. But fresh stock should only be frozen and thawed ONCE. In other words, if you use frozen stock to make a risotto, you can't then freeze the risotto and defrost it later – too much freezing and thawing results in bacteria breeding. You can use frozen stock to make a meal which is then eaten within a day or two. Alternatively, you can keep the stock in the fridge for a few days and make a variety of meals from it, which you can then freeze.
- Use plastic containers to freeze the stock and don't use them for anything else (500 ml is a handy portion size for most recipes).

Tip

THE SMART COOK always has some clear broth in the freezer. If you're short on time and the cupboard is bare, just defrost the broth, bring it to the boil, then throw in a handful of fine noodles or couscous for an instant, tasty meal suitable for all ages, from babies up.

The following stock recipes are very basic. Feel free to add fresh herbs, cloves of garlic, bay leaves, peppercorns and/or any leftover vegetables for a stronger flavour.

Simple Chicken Stock

RECIPE INGREDIENTS

1 roast barbecue chicken carcass or 1 kg chicken bones (from the butcher or chicken shop) / 1 onion, whole / 2 cloves garlic, whole / 2 carrots, whole / 1 stick celery, quartered / 1 tomato, whole / 2 litres water

Put everything into the open pressure cooker and bring to the boil. Close lid, bring to full pressure, then reduce to low heat. Set timer and cook for 20 minutes. Cold water release.

Strain the liquid into a bowl, and discard the chicken bones and vegetables. Refrigerate the liquid and, once it's cooled, skim off any fat that congeals on the surface. Freeze in portions.

Simple Beef Stock

RECIPE INGREDIENTS

1 tbsp olive oil / 1 kg beef bones from butcher or supermarket (a cheap cut of meat like chuck or casserole steak, cut into cubes, is also fine) / 1 onion, whole / 2 cloves garlic, whole / 2 carrots, whole / 1 stick celery / 1 tomato, whole / 2 litres water

Lightly oil a baking tray. Toss the beef bones and vegetables in the oil until coated, then bake in a hot oven for 20 minutes until browned. (The browning is an important part of the process.) Put it all into the pressure cooker with the water, bring to pressure and then reduce to low heat. Set timer and cook for 20 minutes. Cold water release. Strain the liquid and refrigerate. Skim off any fat that congeals on the surface. Freeze in portions.

soups and
side dishes

Essential Chicken Soup

This soup will change your life. I mean it! If there's one thing you get out of this book – please, let it be this. My husband learnt it from his mother Marija, and passed it on to me. Whether it comes from Croatian babas, or Jewish mamas, or just your garden variety Australian mums, this clear chicken soup has been scientifically proven to be good for all sorts of ailments. Scientists can't really figure out why. It just works.

I make this soup at least twice a week. I keep the clear liquid aside to make risotto, chicken noodle soup (for toddlers) and chicken couscous (for babies). I keep some of the chicken meat aside to make chicken salad or curry the next day. But first up, I serve the chicken, vegies and a ladle-full of clear broth as a hearty, classy meal in itself. Great for freezing.

RECIPE INGREDIENTS
6 chicken thighs (more tender than breasts) / 1 onion, whole 1 carrot, whole / 1 potato, halved / 1 celery stick, whole (if there's one in the fridge) / 1 zucchini, whole / 1 tomato, whole (also not essential but gives a nice flavour and colour) / enough water to fill the pressure cooker up to ⅔ full / 6–7 whole peppercorns (if they're in the pantry) / 2 tsp salt / 1 tsp powdered chicken stock

Bung it all in the cooker, bring it up to full pressure, then reduce to low heat. Set timer and cook for 15 minutes. Both natural and cold water release are fine.

Pea and Ham Soup

There are all sorts of ways to make this winter classic, but this is my favourite. The key is to make your stock first (in a pressure cooker it takes only 40 minutes as opposed to two hours). Then you can either keep going and make the soup, or you can freeze the stock and make the soup later.

I usually get two or three ham hocks when they're on special at the supermarket deli, make a big batch of stock and freeze it. Then I know that on a cold winter's day, a perfect pea and ham soup is only 10 minutes away.

STEP 1: HAM STOCK INGREDIENTS
1 tbsp olive oil / 1 onion, cut into four / 2 tsp crushed garlic / 1 celery stick (if you've got it) / 1 big ham hock (from the butcher or supermarket deli section) / 5 peppercorns

Heat a splash of olive oil in the open pressure cooker and fry the onions, garlic and celery. Add the hock and peppercorns, cover completely with cold water and close the lid. Turn the heat up high and bring to high pressure. Reduce to low heat, set your timer, and cook for 40 minutes. Natural release. Take the ham hock out and remove the meat for use in the soup. Strain the rest of the liquid and set aside to use as the basis for the soup.

STEP 2: SOUP INGREDIENTS

1 tbsp olive oil / 1 tbsp butter / 1 onion, finely chopped / 2 tsp crushed garlic / 1 carrot, finely chopped or grated / 1 stalk celery, finely chopped / 1.75 litres of ham stock (or 2 litres if you want a more liquid soup) / 500 g packet of split green peas / ham pieces from the ham hock

Heat the oil and butter in the open pressure cooker, then fry onion, garlic, carrot and celery for 5 minutes. Add the ham stock and the peas and turn heat up to high. Important: keep stirring the mixture until it comes to the boil, otherwise the peas stick to the bottom. Once the soup reaches boiling point, close lid and bring to high pressure. Then, reduce heat to lowest possible setting to maintain high pressure, set your timer, and cook for 10 minutes. Natural release. Put a blending wand through the soup until it's your desired consistency. Add salt to taste.

Tip

THE BUSY COOK can choose not to bother making the ham stock separately. Just stick it all in together and remove the ham hocks once the soup is cooked.

209

Leek and Potato Soup

RECIPE INGREDIENTS

1 tbsp butter / 1 tbsp olive oil / 2 leeks, sliced / 2 tsp crushed garlic / 3 cups chicken stock (either clear chicken broth, liquid chicken stock, or in a pinch, a couple of stock cubes in boiling water) / 4 medium potatoes, each cut into 8 pieces / ½ cup chopped ham or cooked bacon bits (optional) / salt.

Heat butter and oil in pressure cooker, then fry leeks and garlic gently for 10 minutes or until soft. Add stock, potatoes and ham or bacon bits. Close lid, bring to high pressure. Reduce to low heat, set timer and cook on high pressure for 12 minutes. Release can be either cold water or natural, depending on your time constraints. Blend to smooth consistency, add salt to taste. Serve with crusty brown rolls or toasted Turkish bread.

THE FRUGAL COOK wastes nothing. Save vegetable scraps, leftover herbs and chicken and meat bones to turn into delicious home-made stock. The more you put into a stock, the more flavour it has. So rather than throw away that barbecue chicken carcass or the tough ends of celery, put it into a special stock bag in the freezer.

One-Packet Lentil and Vegetable Soup

I call this my one-packet lentil soup because it's a great way to use up those clear packets of lentils that seem to accumulate in my pantry during a health-kick. One whole packet makes up a very big batch of soup that will keep you going for weeks! (Just make sure that you don't fill the pressure cooker more than half-way.)

This is a really easy, healthy recipe that can be varied depending on what's in your fridge and pantry. I often add a couple of teaspoons of curry powder if it's in the middle of winter and it's also nice with lamb – just brown the meat quickly on both sides before adding the other ingredients. You can also halve the amount of lentils used and bump up the vegie content. (If you decide to add a tin of chopped tomatoes, make sure you add it last, and just place the tomatoes gently on top of the rest of the mix so they don't touch the bottom and burn.)

RECIPE INGREDIENTS
1 tbsp olive oil / 1 large onion, finely chopped / 1 tsp crushed garlic / 3 carrots, cut into small cubes / 1 large potato, cut into small cubes / 1 stick celery, chopped / 375 g packet brown lentils / 3 litres chicken stock

In an open pressure cooker, heat the oil and sauté the onions, garlic and carrots for a few minutes. Add the rest of the ingredients and close the lid. Bring to high pressure, then reduce to low heat. Set timer and cook for 12 minutes. Natural release.

Healthy Mashed Potato

Is there such a thing? Mashed potato is the ultimate comfort food – soft, creamy and fluffy. But with all that starch and fat, it's not all that healthy. My solution is to make like a drug dealer, and 'cut' it 50/50 with cauliflower. The result is very similar in look and taste, and I actually prefer the texture because it's not as stiff and starchy as 100 per cent spud.

I make big batches of this mash and freeze it. Mainly, I use it as a topping on my shepherd's pie, or as a vegetable side dish. When the kids were babies, I froze it in ice-cube trays for them. They still love it – and they still haven't twigged they're eating a hidden vegetable, the cauliflower. On desperate nights, I defrost a tub of it, mix in some grated cheese and tuna and serve it with some peas or steamed broccoli.

RECIPE INGREDIENTS
4 large potatoes, cut into small pieces (8 if it's a medium-size spud, into 16 if it's a big one) / 1 cauliflower, cut into similar size pieces (with as little of the stalk as possible) / ½ cup milk / butter and salt to taste.

Put about 2 cups of water into the pressure cooker, add vegetables, and close lid. Bring to high pressure, reduce to low heat, and set timer to 8 minutes. Cold water release. Drain vegetables, and put back into cooker. Add butter, milk and salt, then mash or blend before serving. Divide leftovers into portions and freeze. Option: Add some chopped onion at the start of the recipe.

' Pressure Cookers.

ed uses for this fine

kitchen equipment

to-day !

Stainless Steel

ou'll find a hundred u

ddition to your kitch

Eggplant and Tomato Compote

Is it a side dish? Is it a spread? Is it a sauce or a soup? In Croatia, they call this super-healthy Mediterranean dish *su su* (pronounced *shu shu*) and it is served year round in all sorts of ways.

In the Australian summer, it is a perfect chutney to be served alongside cold cuts like ham and turkey. It's also one of my family's favourite sandwich spreads – get some fresh rye bread, spread it with avocado, then top with pureed su su.

In winter, heat it up to make a delicious soup or pasta sauce. And all year round, we enjoy it as a healthy, natural alternative to tomato sauce, adding it to classics like pork, chicken schnitzel and meatballs. You don't have to use all the vegetables listed here: the only essentials are the onions, garlic, eggplants and tomatoes. Very little water is used in this recipe because a lot comes out of the tomatoes and eggplant.

RECIPE INGREDIENTS
1 tbsp olive oil / 2 brown onions, chopped / 1 tbsp paprika / 5 tsp crushed garlic / 2 eggplants, sliced and chopped / ½ cup water / 1 zucchini, sliced / 1 capsicum, chopped / handful of mushrooms, chopped / 6 fresh tomatoes, chopped / salt

Heat the oil in the cooker and fry the onions, paprika, garlic and eggplant until soft (about 4–5 minutes). Add the water and bring to boiling point. Add all the other vegetables, placing the tomatoes on top last, and close the lid. Make sure the pressure cooker is no more than two-thirds full. Bring to full pressure. (Note: because of the large amount of cold vegetables used, the cooker may take longer to heat up and come to pressure.) Reduce to low heat, then set the timer and cook for 15 minutes. Natural release. Open lid, stir and add salt. Drain off excess water if desired. For babies, puree mixture with blending wand. For sandwiches, wraps and pasta, also puree. As a soup or side dish, mash with a fork to break up the larger pieces, or serve as is. Can be served warm or cold.

rice and pasta

Steamed White Rice

Rice is very easy to cook in a pressure cooker. Depending what type of rice you use (short, medium or long grain), it takes between 4 and 7 minutes to cook. The recipe below is for long grain rice, including jasmine and basmati, which is the fastest to cook. The ratio of white rice to water is always 1:1.5. So regardless of how much rice you're cooking, just make sure you add 1 ½ times that amount of water. One cup of uncooked white rice = 3 cups cooked.

Pour 3 cups of water into the pressure cooker and bring to the boil. While the water is heating, wash 2 cups of white long grain rice in a strainer until the water runs clear. Add rice to boiling water, close lid and bring to full pressure. Reduce to low heat, set timer, and cook for 4 minutes. Natural release. Remove lid and fluff rice with a fork – all the water should have been absorbed with no need to strain it.

Steamed White Rice and Vegetables

While you're at it, you may as well throw some vegies in the pot, too. As long as they're cut to the right size, they'll take the same time to cook as the rice, saving you an extra pot. Then you can just add some defrosted curry or stew, or whatever else you have in the freezer – and voilà! – a complete meal in 4 minutes.

If you're cooking a denser vegetable like carrot with the rice, it will have to be sliced quite finely so that it cooks in 4 minutes. A less dense vegetable like broccoli, which takes less time to cook, can be the same size it would be if you were boiling it. A vegetable with a high percentage of water, like zucchini, cooks in a very short period of time and may get soggy when cooked with the rice, so stick to the firmer vegies.

Steamed Brown Rice

Brown rice is healthier for you because it still has the oil-rich husk attached to it, and it is loaded with vitamin B and other nutrients. It has a nuttier flavour and a slightly chewy texture and takes longer to cook.

Brown rice requires a higher rice to water ratio of 1:2. So, however much rice you intend to cook, make sure you have twice as much water to cook it in. The procedure is the same for cooking white rice, except you don't have to rinse it first, and of course it has a longer cooking time. One cup of uncooked brown rice = 4 cups cooked.

PRESSURE COOKING TIMES FOR RICE

RICE	TIME	PROPORTIONS
Long Grain Rice *including basmati and jasmine*	4 minutes	1 cup rice to 1½ cups water
Short Grain Rice *including arborio*	7 minutes	1 cup rice to 1½ cups water
Medium Grain Rice *including Calrose*	7 minutes	1 cup rice to 1½ cups water
Brown Rice *long grain*	12 minutes	1 cup rice to 2 cups water
Brown Rice *medium and short grain*	15 minutes	1 cup rice to 2 cups water
Wild Rice	20 minutes	1 cup rice to 4 cups water

The Amazing 7-Minute Risotto

I love risotto, but before I got my pressure cooker I hadn't made it for 15 years. That was the last time I'd had a free 50 minutes to stand over a pot stirring in stock one drop at a time. Well, forget all that mucking about. Just bung everything in the cooker, bring it to high pressure, and a mere 7 minutes later you'll have perfect risotto. It freezes well, too. Timing's very important with this recipe – you need to reduce the pressure quickly after cooking, so the rice doesn't overcook.

RECIPE INGREDIENTS
1 tsp olive oil / 1 small onion, finely chopped / 1 cup arborio or other short grain rice / 2 cups chopped mushrooms / 2¼ cups chicken stock and bits of chopped cooked chicken / ⅓ cup parmesan cheese / 1 cup frozen peas

In cooker, heat oil over medium heat. Sauté onion for 4–5 minutes or until soft. Add rice and cook, stirring often, until light brown. Add mushrooms and stock. Turn heat up to high, then keep stirring until almost boiling. Close lid and bring to high pressure. Reduce to low heat, set timer, and cook for 7 minutes. Cold water release. Stir in parmesan, frozen peas and chopped cooked chicken, then serve or freeze. (There's enough heat in the risotto at that point to warm the chicken and cook the peas, and they'll stay bright green.) Options: Also try with salmon, tuna, or fresh asparagus.

Cooking Pasta in a Pressure Cooker

There's no big time saving to cooking pasta in a pressure cooker on its own, but it works really well in combination dishes where you've got a sauce and other ingredients in the cooker as well. The main thing to remember is that when cooking pasta in a pressure cooker, you only need enough liquid to barely cover the pasta, so it absorbs it completely. A few other rules:

- Only use dry pasta. Fresh pasta is not suitable because it cooks too quickly and disintegrates.
- Thin spaghetti is not suitable. Thick spaghetti is fine. Break it into smaller pieces before adding to the pot and stir to break up any strands stuck together.
- Always add a tablespoon of olive oil to stop the pasta foaming as it cooks.
- Never fill the cooker past halfway mark when cooking pasta.
- Always use natural release.

Tip

THE FRUGAL COOK saves time and money by doing the supermarket shopping after 9 pm, when the aisles are empty and a lot of things are on special.

105/-

95/-

8

One Pot Pasta Chilli Con Carne

This is a great example of how you can use a pressure cooker to make a perfect pasta combination dish. It's fast, tasty and you don't have a separate pasta pot to wash up. If you're making it for young children, you can leave out the chilli and simply make it a savoury mince, or add a bit of curry powder or paste for a different flavour. Celery and capsicum are also good in this recipe, if you have them on hand. Chicken or beef stock is fine to use instead of water, as long as there's enough liquid to just cover the pasta.

RECIPE INGREDIENTS
500 g mince / 1 onion, chopped / 2 tsp crushed garlic / 1 tbsp olive oil / 1 tin crushed tomatoes / 3 tbsp tomato paste / 1 cup chopped capsicum / 420 g tin kidney or other beans, drained and rinsed / 1 tsp chilli powder / 2 cups small-shape pasta, uncooked / salt to taste / 1 cup grated cheese

Heat the oil in the cooker and brown mince over medium heat, along with onions and garlic. Pour off any liquid once cooked. Add the beans, capsicum, chilli, tomatoes and tomato paste and stir well. Add pasta, with enough water to just cover it. Close the lid, bring to pressure, then reduce heat. Cook for 6 minutes. Natural release. Salt to taste and sprinkle cheese on top. Serve. Freezes well.

main meals

Easy Beef Curry

When I am on a mission to convert people to the cult of pressure cooking, this is one of my show stoppers, along with risotto. It is SO delicious, and SO easy, that people's eyes immediately glaze over and they become willing subjects. The key is adding banana or pineapple – the sweetness takes the sting out of the curry, and it's a great way to get kids used to something a little more exotic.

RECIPE INGREDIENTS

1 tbsp olive oil / 1 large onion, chopped / 2 tsp crushed garlic / 2 tsp curry powder or curry paste (I use vindaloo paste in a jar) / 1 cup beef stock / 2 tbsp fruit chutney / 1 apple, chopped / 1 banana, chopped / 1 kg diced beef (blade or chuck) / 2 tbsp tomato paste / 200 ml light coconut milk (or coconut cream if you prefer a thicker consistency)

Heat oil in open pressure cooker. Add onions and garlic and cook until soft. Add curry powder or paste, cook for a minute or two, then add stock, chutney, apple and banana. Stir well. Heat some oil in a separate pot and brown the diced beef. Transfer the beef to the pressure cooker and stir the mix well. Increase heat to almost boiling point. Put the tomato paste on top, but do not stir (tomato products tend to burn if they're at the bottom of the pot). Close the lid. Bring to high pressure, then reduce to low heat. Set timer and cook for 10 minutes. Natural release. Stir in coconut milk to taste. Serve with rice and steamed greens. Freeze any leftover curry in portions.

Option 1 : To make curried beef puffs with leftover curry, use a slotted spoon (so that liquid drains off) and place a spoonful of beef curry in a circle of puff pastry. Pinch the edges together to form a parcel, brush with melted butter and cook in moderate oven until golden brown.

Option 2: Add some carrot and potato (cut into small pieces) at the same time as the tomatoes. If you like a sweeter curry, you can also add some tinned pineapple and juice, and more banana.

Tip

THE GREEN COOK uses pressure cooking rather than regular methods because it uses less energy and leaves a smaller carbon footprint.

Bolognese Sauce with Mushrooms

I went to Bologna once, to the book fair, but I never met anyone I could actually say *Grazie* to for this glorious Italian creation. It's the most versatile sauce I know. Add some chilli and it morphs into a treat for spicy adult palates. Serve it with a green salad and a glass of wine if you get an unexpected drop-in for lunch. Puree it for babies. Add some grated carrots and zucchini and your fussy toddler will be none the wiser. Try it with capsicum, sun-dried tomatoes or eggplant. I always add mushrooms to mine – because I love mushrooms and there are just not enough opportunities in the world to eat more mushrooms. Be creative. Make lots of it and freeze it and you'll never have to order in junk food.

RECIPE INGREDIENTS
1 tbsp olive oil / 1 large onion, chopped / 2 tsp crushed garlic / 1 kg beef mince / 2 handfuls of button mushrooms, chopped / ½ cup stock (ham or beef is best, but any will do) / 2 x 420 g tins of diced tomatoes with added herbs / 2 tbsp tomato paste / salt

Heat olive oil in the open pressure cooker and fry onions and garlic for 5 minutes. Add the mince and cook until browned. Then add the mushrooms and cook for another few minutes. Add the stock, tinned tomatoes and tomato paste. Gently place the tinned tomatoes and tomato paste on top of the mixture and do not stir through. (Tomatoes contain sugar and can sometimes burn if they touch the

227

cooking surface.) Close lid, turn heat up high and bring to high pressure. Reduce temperature to low heat, set timer, and cook for 8 minutes. Natural release. Stir well, add salt to taste and serve with pasta or rice.

THE HEALTHY COOK throws a handful of broccoli, zucchini, beans or asparagus into the same pot 5 minutes before the rice or pasta is ready. Saves on the washing up too!

Osso Bucco

This classic Italian dish is perfect for pressure cooking. Before, I never had the time to make it because it normally takes hours, but with a pressure cooker it's done in 20 minutes. The name literally means 'bone with a hole in it', and the bone marrow is an important part of the rich flavour.

RECIPE INGREDIENTS

1 tbsp olive oil / 8 osso bucco veal shanks (about 1.5 kg) / 2 brown onions, chopped / 2 tsp crushed garlic / 2 sticks celery, chopped / 2 carrots, diced / 1 cup white wine / 1 cup beef stock / ½ cup balsamic vinegar / 2 tbsp tomato paste / ½ cup flour / salt

Heat the oil in the pressure cooker and brown meat on both sides. Set aside. Add onions and garlic to pressure cooker and cook until soft. Put the meat back in. Add celery, carrots, wine, beef stock and vinegar. Turn heat up, and stir until simmering. Place tomato paste on top (don't stir, as tomato products tend to burn if they touch the bottom of the pot). Then close the lid and bring to high pressure. Reduce to low heat. Set timer and cook for 20 minutes. Natural release. Add salt to taste. Serve with mashed potatoes, rice or pasta.

Tip

THE HEALTHY COOK uses pressure rather than regular methods because it locks in the nutrients through super-fast cooking times and a sealed environment.

Beef and Vegetable Pie

I make this fabulous pie in two stages: first, the filling, which I freeze in portions or set aside in the fridge until I'm ready to bake the pie. The second stage is putting the puff pastry crust on top and baking in the oven, which is something a partner or older kids can easily do if you're at work. Once you've got the filling made, you're only 25 minutes away from serving up a delicious home-made pie with fluffy golden pastry. You can also use it as the filling for individual pasties.

RECIPE INGREDIENTS
2 tbsp olive oil / 500 g beef (chuck or blade) cut into small pieces / 1 onion, chopped / 2 tsp crushed garlic / 1 stick of celery, chopped / 2 cups chopped mushrooms / 1 cup beef stock / splash of red wine (optional) / 2 carrots, chopped / 2 tbsp tomato paste / 1 cup frozen peas / 1 sheet puff pastry / 1 tbsp melted butter

Stage 1: Heat half the oil in open pressure cooker and brown meat. Then, heat the rest of the oil in a separate pan and cook onions, garlic and celery until soft. Add mushrooms and cook for another five minutes. Add the onion and mushroom mix to the pressure cooker, then add beef stock (and wine if you want) and carrots. Stir until it starts to simmer. Place the tomato paste on top (don't stir it through – tomato products tend to burn if they touch the bottom of the pot at high heat). Close the lid and bring to high pressure. Then reduce to low heat and set your timer for 7 minutes. Natural release. When you take the lid off, stir in the frozen peas – they will cook in the remaining heat.

Stage 2: Preheat the oven to 200°C. Pour filling into a pie dish and cover with a sheet of puff pastry. Brush pastry with melted butter, and bake in oven until golden brown, around 25 minutes. If you have any mix left over, use it to make little beef parcels (or pasties) with quarter sheets of puff pastry.

Tip

THE SMART COOK thickens a sauce or stew by adding a butter/flour paste. While the dish is cooking, melt a tablespoon of butter in a small pan, add a tablespoon of flour, mix to a smooth paste, and cook for a few minutes. When the lid comes off the pressure cooker, stir in the paste and return the whole thing to the heat. Bring it all to a simmer and the mixture will thicken.

Goulash

This is the first recipe I made when I bought the old Hawkins pressure cooker and it's still one of my favourites. The recipe was in the original booklet that came with the cooker, but every time I made it, I changed it a bit. You can serve it with rice, but I prefer to use the pasta spirals – it goes a lot further and you can mix it all together in a big serving dish. It's quick and easy, and great to serve with salad if you've got people over for lunch.

RECIPE INGREDIENTS
1 tbsp olive oil / 1 large onion, chopped / 2 tsp crushed garlic / 12 button mushrooms, sliced / 1 kg diced beef or veal / 1 ¼ cups beef stock / 2 tsp paprika / 2 tsp Dijon or seeded mustard (optional) / 3 tbsp tomato paste / 3 tbsp light sour cream / 4 cups pasta spirals / salt

Heat oil in the pressure cooker and cook onions, garlic, mushrooms and meat. Stir until the meat is browned on all sides. Add stock, paprika and mustard. Give it a good stir until it's all mixed through and close to simmering. Place the tomato paste on top. (Don't stir; tomato products contain sugar and tend to burn if they touch the bottom of the pot.) Close the lid, and bring to full pressure. Reduce to low heat, set timer, and cook for 8 minutes. While you're waiting, put the pasta on to boil. When the timer goes off, release pressure slowly (natural release), then stir in the sour cream, and salt to taste. Drain pasta, mix with goulash, and serve. Freeze leftovers.

Swordfish with Potato and Parsley

This is the fastest, easiest and most delicious fish meal ever. Swordfish is a perfect fish for the pressure cooker because it is firm and thick, and does not tend to overcook like lighter fish. Luckily, it takes about the same time to cook as the potato, which means this is a very easy one-pot meal to make. It uses very few ingredients and the parsley gives it a beautiful fresh, summery taste.

The recipe comes from my mother-in-law, who makes this most Fridays as a delicious fish soup. My children love it, so I was thrilled at how easily it adapted to the pressure cooker. You can add or reduce the amount of water, depending on how thick you want the consistency. You can also use white rice instead of potato (just make sure you rinse it thoroughly first). But don't skimp on the parsley!

RECIPE INGREDIENTS

2 medium potatoes, cut into thin (½ centimetre) slices / 2 swordfish steaks, cut into bite-sized chunks / 1 large bunch parsley, enough for two big handfuls, chopped finely (flat-leaf parsley is best, but the ordinary variety is fine) / 2 cups water / 2 tbsp olive oil / 1 tsp crushed garlic / 1 tsp salt

Place all ingredients into the cooker and bring to boiling point. Close lid, bring to full pressure, then reduce to low heat. Set timer and cook for 7 minutes. Cold water release, then stir. That's it!

PREPARATION TIME *10 minutes*
PRESSURE *cooking time: 8 minutes*
REGULAR *cooking time: 40 minutes*

Baba's One-Minute Summer Prawns

On the rare occasion that busy people manage to host a dinner party, this is the perfect recipe – it looks special, but it's ridiculously fast, fresh and easy to make. Plus, it's suitable for freezing if you want to keep it for more pedestrian occasions.

The key to it is lots of garlic, lots of fresh parsley, and boiling up the prawn heads for stock instead of throwing them out. You also need to make sure the mixture is very hot before locking the lid in place so that the cooker comes to full pressure very quickly and the prawns don't overcook.

In my mother-in-law's native Croatia, this dish is cooked with the prawn heads and skins intact. This is how she's adapted it for Australia, and how I've adapted it for pressure cooking. (Naturally, she grows her own parsley, but most of us will find it quicker to buy it at the shops.)

RECIPE INGREDIENTS

1 kg king green prawns / ½ tsp vegetable stock powder / 2 tbsp olive oil / 5 tsp crushed garlic / 1 large bunch of parsley, enough for two big handfuls, chopped finely (flat-leaf Continental parsley is best, but the ordinary variety is also fine) / 2 tsp cornflour / 1 cup white wine

Peel the prawns, leaving the tails on but removing the heads. Boil the heads in a small amount of water, just enough to cover them, with some salt and the stock powder. In the pressure cooker, heat

234

the oil until very hot. Then add the garlic, parsley and prawns, stir-frying for 30 seconds (it should be hot enough to be sizzling). Mix the cornflour with the white wine, stir until dissolved, then add to the pressure cooker. Strain the prawn stock and stir 1 cup of it into the pressure cooker (freeze any leftover stock for later use in prawn curries, etc). Close the pressure cooker, and it should come to pressure almost immediately. Set timer and cook for 1 minute. Fast release in cold water. Serve with rice and green salad.

Alternative: add a teaspoon of chilli powder and/or some diced tomatoes for a different kind of sauce. If adding tomatoes, reduce the amount of stock and wine used so the mixture is not too liquid.

LOW PRESSURE *cooking time: 7 minutes*
HIGH PRESSURE *cooking time: 5 minutes*
REGULAR *cooking time: 15 minutes*

Simple Salmon

This recipe gives you a good opportunity to experiment with the low pressure setting on your cooker, if it has one. Low pressure is perfect for fish, because it's gentler – fish is easily overcooked if you blast it. But if you only have a high pressure setting, don't worry – this recipe works fine on high pressure too, you just need to reduce the time slightly. The only difference is that the salmon will be cooked right through, instead of having the tender centre you'll get on the low setting. The lemon, vinegar and parsley in this recipe give the salmon a fresh, tangy flavour, which makes it perfect to serve hot or cold.

RECIPE INGREDIENTS
½ cup water / ½ cup white wine vinegar / 2 tsp crushed garlic / 1 onion, sliced / handful of parsley, chopped finely (either flat-leaf or curly is fine) / 2 salmon fillets, about 25 mm thick / 2 lemons

Put water, vinegar, garlic, onion and parsley into open cooker and bring to boiling point. Place salmon into cooker. Cut 1 lemon into thin slices and arrange on top. Close lid, put on low pressure setting and bring to full pressure. Reduce heat, set timer and cook for 6 minutes. Cold water release. Remove salmon and discard the rest of the ingredients. Season with salt, pepper and a squeeze of lemon.

Pork Chops with Honey Mustard Sauce

The star of this dish is the sweet, creamy sauce, which tastes just as good with chicken breasts. Pork loin works well too, seared then cut into slices before pressure cooking. Note: I use canola oil with this recipe rather than olive oil because you can heat it to a higher temperature. That makes it good for quickly browning the meat on the outside without cooking it on the inside.

RECIPE INGREDIENTS
2 tbsp canola oil / 4 pork chops / 1 onion, chopped / 2 tsp crushed garlic / 1 cup chicken stock / 2 tbsp Dijon mustard / 2 tbsp honey / 2 tbsp light sour cream / ½ tsp salt

Heat the oil until it is very hot, then quickly brown the chops on both sides and set aside. Add the onions and garlic to the cooker, and stir until soft. Add the stock and mustard and stir until smooth. Put the chops back in the cooker, close the lid and bring to pressure. Reduce to low heat, set timer and cook for 8 minutes. Natural release. Transfer the chops to a serving dish, then add honey to the sauce in the cooker. Turn heat up high and simmer for 10 minutes or until the sauce starts to thicken and caramelise. Remove from heat and add sour cream and salt, stirring until smooth. If you have time, return chops to cooker and allow to sit in the creamy sauce for a few minutes before serving. Otherwise, pour sauce over chops immediately and serve with steamed greens and mashed potato/cauliflower.

Spicy Pork Fillet

I found this recipe in the instruction booklet of my old Hawkins and changed it from pork chops to fillet. The use of soy sauce must have made it quite daring and 'spicy' for its time! With a bit of tweaking, it's become a good tasty stand-by because it uses basic ingredients that are always in the pantry, and are very quick to throw together.
Note: I use canola oil with this recipe rather than olive oil because you can heat it to a higher temperature. That makes it good for quickly browning the meat on the outside without cooking it on the inside.

RECIPE INGREDIENTS
2 tbsp canola oil / 500 g lean pork fillet / 1 onion, chopped / 2 tsp crushed garlic / 2 tbsp honey / 2 tbsp soy sauce / 1 tbsp tomato paste (or 1 frozen cube, defrosted) / squeeze of lemon juice / 1 tsp Dijon mustard / 4 tbsp red wine vinegar

Heat the oil in the cooker until quite hot and quickly brown the fillet on both sides. Set aside. When it cools, cut into slices. Add onion and garlic to the cooker (put in some extra oil if needed), and fry until soft. In a bowl, mix the honey, soy, tomato paste, lemon juice, mustard and vinegar, then add to the cooker along with the chops. Close lid, bring to pressure, then reduce to low heat. Set timer and cook for 8 minutes. Natural release. Salt to taste and serve with boiled rice and steamed greens.

Chicken and Vegetables with Couscous

RECIPE INGREDIENTS

1 kg chicken drumsticks / 1 large onion, chopped / 2 tsp crushed garlic / handful of flat-leaf parsley, chopped finely / 2 carrots, cut into 3 cm chunks / 1 capsicum, chopped / handful of button mushrooms, chopped / 400 g tin crushed tomatoes / ½ cup chicken broth / 1 zucchini, sliced / ½ cup couscous

Put all the ingredients except zucchini and couscous into cooker. Close lid and bring to high pressure. Set timer, reduce heat and cook for 8 minutes. Quick release (so that food temperature stays high despite drop in pressure). Add zucchini and couscous and wait for couscous to be absorbed (around 5 minutes). Season to taste.

Garlic Lamb Shanks with Rosemary

This is a classic Australian dish with three ingredients that are pure magic together: lamb, rosemary and garlic. Usually it takes hours, but with a pressure cooker, it's on the table in no time.

RECIPE INGREDIENTS
1 tbsp olive oil / 1 kg lamb shanks / 6 cloves whole garlic, or six teaspoons crushed or pureed / ½ cup chicken stock / splash of red wine / a few sprigs of fresh rosemary, chopped / 1 tbsp tomato paste / 1 tbsp butter / 1 tbsp plain flour / 1 tbsp balsamic vinegar

Heat the olive oil until quite hot, then quickly brown the shanks on both sides. Reduce heat and add garlic, cooking until soft, and making sure not to burn it. Add the stock, wine and rosemary. Stir to mix. Place tomato paste on top of the shanks (so as not to burn), turn up heat and close lid. Bring to high pressure. Reduce heat, set timer, and cook for 30 minutes. Natural release. Remove lamb shanks and place in a serving dish. In a separate pan, melt the butter and stir in the flour to make a paste. Cook the paste for 3–4 minutes. Return the cooker to the heat, uncovered, and bring to the simmer. Whisk in the paste until the sauce thickens, then add the balsamic vinegar. Pour sauce over the shanks, and serve with mixed vegies.

Bake everything

in's *Self-Raisi*
FLOU

ovides happiness
hen those Cakes,

Jolly Green Meatballs

These meatballs are so full of hidden vegetables and fresh herbs that they look like they've been picked fresh from the garden! They're healthy enough to be a meal in themselves, but you can also combine them with spaghetti and pasta sauce, or drop them into a bowl of clear chicken or beef broth (see pages 204–205).

This recipe is a great way to introduce babies to the taste of herbs like basil and parsley and, when they grow into fussy toddlers, a clever way to get vegetables into them by stealth. I make them in bulk about once a month and always have them in the freezer for an instant, popular kids' meal.

This is one recipe where I prefer to use a food processor (actually, it's the very basic one that came with my blending wand) because with small meatballs, it is necessary to have all the ingredients finely chopped.

RECIPE INGREDIENTS
1 onion / 2 carrots / 2 tsp crushed garlic /handful of fresh parsley / handful of fresh basil / handful fresh baby spinach leaves (optional)/ 1 egg / 1 tsp salt / ½ cup flour / 1 kg beef mince / 2 cups canola oil

Put the onion, carrots, garlic, herbs, baby spinach (if using), egg, salt and flour into a food processor until it is finely chopped and mixed. (Alternatively, chop all the ingredients by hand and mix.) Combine mixture with the mince and mix thoroughly. Using a teaspoon, shape the mixture into small balls. Roll in flour to soak up excess moisture and place on a tray. Heat several centimetres of canola oil in a saucepan until very hot, then fry meatballs, about 8 at a time, for 3–4 minutes or until crunchy and golden-green. Place on paper towel to cool, then freeze in bags of 10. Makes about 50 meatballs.

Note: meatballs can also be placed on an oven tray lined with baking paper and baked in a moderate oven until golden-green and cooked.

Meatloaf Muffins

These are an excellent place to hide vegetables and the cupcake-size portions make them perfect for babies and toddlers. If you don't have a tray with muffin moulds in it, you can also use large paper patty cases. Make sure you let the muffins cool before serving, because they tend to be a bit sloppy when they're straight out of the oven.

RECIPE INGREDIENTS
1 onion / 1 carrot / 1 zucchini / 500 g pork and veal mince / ½ cup breadcrumbs (plain or multigrain) / 1 egg, lightly beaten / 1 tsp crushed garlic / 1 tsp paprika / ½ cup tomato sauce / 1 cup grated tasty cheese

Preheat oven to 170°C. Lightly grease a 12-mould muffin tray. Grate the onion, carrot and zucchini. In a bowl, combine the remaining ingredients, except the tomato sauce and cheese, and mix thoroughly by hand. (I put it all into a plastic bag without holes in it, and mix it by squeezing the bag. That way you don't have to actually touch the mixture.) Spoon the mixture into the individual muffin moulds and press into place, making sure the mixture does not go all the way to the top of the mould. Cover with aluminium foil and bake for 15 minutes. Remove foil, glaze top of muffins with tomato sauce and sprinkle with grated cheese. Return to the oven and bake uncovered for another 15 minutes. Allow to cool. To freeze, wrap muffins individually in aluminium foil and put in an airtight freezer bag.

Vegetarian Muffins

RECIPE INGREDIENTS
1 zucchini, grated / 1 carrot, grated / 2 x 125 g tin corn kernels, drained / 1 cup grated cheese / 2 ½ cups self-raising flour / 2 eggs / 125 g butter / 1 cup milk

Preheat oven to 200°C. Lightly oil a muffin tray. Combine zucchini, carrot, corn and cheese in a bowl. Add flour and stir well. Whisk eggs, butter and milk in a separate bowl, and stir into the flour mixture. Spoon mixture into muffin moulds and bake for 20 minutes or until golden brown. Allow to cool. To freeze, wrap muffins individually in aluminium foil and put in an airtight freezer bag.

desserts

Golden Syrup Pudding

Growing up, the best thing about winter was Mum's golden syrup pudding made in the pressure cooker. This retro Australian treat uses only a few ingredients and has the added wow-factor of being self-saucing.

RECIPE INGREDIENTS

1 cup golden syrup / ¾ cup sugar / 4 tbsp butter or margarine, softened at room temperature / 2 eggs / 2 cups self raising flour, sifted / 1 cup milk / 5 cups water

Grease a pudding bowl and pour in the golden syrup. In a mixer, cream sugar and butter. Add eggs one at a time and beat well. Fold in the flour and milk, and mix well. Pour mixture into the pudding bowl and cover (some metal pudding bowls come with their own lock-on lids. If using a china pudding bowl, cover with a layer of baking paper and then aluminium foil. Secure with string around the rim of the bowl. Place bowl into pressure cooker, on top of trivet. Pour in water. Place lid loosely on top and steam for 15 minutes. This allows the mixture to rise. Then secure the lid, bring to high pressure, reduce heat, and cook for 45 minutes. Natural release. Remove bowl and cover. Turn pudding onto plate and serve warm with whipped cream, custard or ice-cream.

Variations: Use jam instead of golden syrup. (You can also layer the jam and pudding mixture.) To make a ginger pudding, add 2 tsp ground ginger and 1 tbsp chopped ginger.

Simple Rice Pudding

Rice pudding cooked the traditional way, in an oven, can take up to 2 hours. But when you're pushed for time, here's a really quick, easy alternative using the pressure cooker. This recipe uses the low pressure setting.

RECIPE INGREDIENTS
½ cup rice / 400 ml tin coconut milk / ¼ cup sugar / 1 cup water / 1 tsp vanilla extract

Mix the rice, coconut milk, sugar and water in a pressure cooker. Close the lid and bring up to full pressure, then lower to low pressure for 20 minutes. Natural release. When the mixture cools to room temperature, stir in vanilla and refrigerate.

Rice Pudding for Rocket Scientists

Okay, so you don't exactly need a uni degree. But this version is slightly more complicated than the simple rice pudding recipe – which means it's not very complicated at all. Another point of difference is that this recipe uses the high pressure setting, as opposed to low, and takes even less time. Compare the two to see which works best for you.

RECIPE INGREDIENTS
1 cup rice / ½ tsp olive oil / 2 ¼ cups water / ⅓ cup honey / ½ cup sugar / 1 cup skim milk / 3 egg yolks / ⅓ cup raisins / 1 tsp vanilla extract / cinnamon, to taste

Combine rice, olive oil and water in pressure cooker. Close lid, bring to high pressure and cook for 8 minutes. Cold water release. Open lid, add honey, sugar, milk and egg yolks. Cook, while stirring, over medium heat for a couple of minutes until mixture thickens. Add raisins and vanilla and sprinkle with cinnamon. Served hot or can be refrigerated.

Lemon Delicious

RECIPE INGREDIENTS
250 g butter, softened at room temperature / 1 cup sugar / 2 eggs /
1 cup self-raising flour, sifted / 2 tbsp lemon zest / ¼ cup lemon juice
/ 1¼ cups boiling water, plus extra

In a mixer, cream the butter with a ¼ cup of the sugar until fluffy.
Lightly beat the eggs, then gradually add them to the mixture, along
with the flour, a little at a time. Finally, add half the lemon zest and
stir through. Pour the mixture into a greased pudding bowl. In a
separate dish, combine the rest of the lemon zest, juice and sugar with
the boiling water. Gently pour the liquid into the pudding bowl, over
the mixture, and cover. (If the pudding bowl does not have a lid, use
a layer of baking paper followed by a layer of aluminium foil. Secure
with string around the rim of the bowl.) Place the bowl onto a trivet
in the pressure cooker, then pour in 5 cups of boiling water. Close
the lid loosely and steam for 15 minutes to allow the rising agent to
work. Then lock the lid in place, bring to high pressure and cook for
10 minutes. Natural release. Serve with cream or ice-cream.

PRESSURE *cooking time: 45 minutes*
REGULAR *cooking time: 1 ½ hours*

Chocolate Pudding

RECIPE INGREDIENTS
125 g butter / ½ cup soft brown sugar / 2 eggs / 60 g melted dark chocolate / 1 cup self-raising flour / 4 cups boiling water

In a mixer, cream the butter and sugar. Lightly beat the eggs in a small bowl and then gradually add them to the mix, along with the flour, a little at a time. Stir in the melted chocolate. Gently pour into a greased pudding bowl and cover. (If the pudding bowl does not have a lid, use a layer of baking paper followed by a layer of aluminium foil. Secure with string around the rim of the bowl.) Place bowl on top of trivet in the pressure cooker and pour in boiling water. Close lid of cooker loosely and steam for 15 minutes to allow rising agent to work. Lock lid in place, bring to high pressure and cook for 30 minutes. Natural release. Serve with strawberries and cream.

endnotes

1   Lyn Craig, Michael Bittman, Jude Brown and Denise Thompson, Social Policy Research Centre, UNSW, 'Managing work and family', SPRC Report, June 2008.

2   Antonia Kidman, 'Wisdom of the Ages', *Sunday Life* magazine, *Sun Herald*, 10 May 2009, pp11–12.

3   Angela Saurine, 'Family meals fall foul of time', *The Daily Telegraph*, 31 March 2008, p8.

4   National Health Survey 2007–08, Australian Bureau of Statistics.

5   Richard Glover, 'In just five minutes a day I can develop a beautiful bustline and become closer to God', *The Sydney Morning Herald*, 5 July 2008, p20.

6   Lyn Craig, 'How do they do it? A time-diary analysis of how working mothers find time for the kids,' Social Policy Research Centre, UNSW, discussion paper No. 136, January 2005.

7   Janelle McCulloch, 'Switching Off', *Sunday Life* magazine, *Sun Herald*, 29 March 2009, pp15–16.

8   Sarah Wilson, 'Ahead of Time', *Sunday Life* magazine, *Sun Herald*, 1 March 2009, p10–12.

9   ibid.

10 Ruth Cowan, *More Work for Mother: The Ironies of Household Technology from the Open Hearth to the Microwave*, Free Association Books, 1989.

11 'Unpaid Work and the Australian Economy, Australian Economic Indicators' (cat. no. 1350), July 2001, Australian Bureau of Statistics.

12 Bettina Arndt, 'Stop putting down the dads', *Herald Sun*, 23 July 2007.

13 Scott Coltrane, 'Men's changing contribution to housework and childcare', Council on Contemporary Families, April 2008.

14 Neil Chethik, *VoiceMale: what husbands really think about their marriage, wives, sex, housework and commitment,* Simon and Schuster, 2008.

15 Barbara Pocock, 'Having a life: work, family, fairness and community in 2000', Centre for Labour Research, Adelaide University, 2001.

16 Pia Schober, 'Family work and selection into parenthood among British couples', London School of Economics, July 2007.

17 Lyn Craig and Pooja Sawrikar, 'Housework and divorce: the division of domestic labour and relationship', Social Policy Research Centre, UNSW, July 2007.

18 Lyn Craig, 'A cross-national comparison of the impact of children on adult time', Social Policy Research Centre, UNSW, discussion paper No. 137, February 2005.

19 Craig and Sawrikar, op. cit.

20 Leonie J. Bloomfield and Gerard A. Kennedy, 'Killing Time: excess free time and men's mortality risk', University of Victoria, 2006.

21 Harriet Alexander, 'Killer study: why men should be dying to do the housework', *The Sydney Morning Herald,* 15 June 2006.

22 Lyn Craig, Michael Bittman, Jude Brown and Denise Thompson, op. cit.

23 Lyn Craig, 'Caring differently: a time use analysis of the type and social context of childcare performed by fathers and by mothers', Social Policy Research Centre, UNSW, discussion paper No. 116, September 2002.

24 Lyn Craig, Michael Bittman, Jude Brown and Denise Thompson, op. cit.

25 Lyn Craig, op. cit.

26 Patricia Reaney, 'Husbands create 7 hours extra housework a week: study', Reuters.com, 4 April 2008.

27 Adele Horin, 'Maternity leave exposes "culture of antagonism"', *The Sydney Morning Herald,* 27 December 2008.

28 Nikki Barrowclough, 'The Hard Yards', *Good Weekend* magazine, *The Sydney Morning Herald,* 18 October 2008, p80.

29 Adele Horin, 'Till dusting do us part', *The Sydney Morning Herald,* 20 September 2008, p31.

30 Barbara Pocock, Natalie Skinner and Philippa Williams, 'Work, life and time: the Australian work and life index 2007', Centre for Work and Life, University of South Australia; Lyn Craig, 'How do they do it? A time-diary analysis of how working mothers find time for the kids', Social Policy Research Centre, UNSW, discussion paper No. 136, January 2005.

31 Brigid Van Wanrooy, *Australia@Work,* Workplace Research Centre, University of Sydney, 2008.

32 Stephen Lunn, 'Dads also hit hard by post-natal depression,' *The Australian,* 17 November 2008.

33 Lyn Craig, 'Father Care, Father Share in International Perspective', Social Policy Research Centre, UNSW, October 2008.

34 Philippa Poole, *The Diaries of Ethel Turner,* Ure Smith, 1979.

35 Joann Vanek, *Keeping Busy: Time spent in housework, United States 1920-1970,* University of Michigan, 1973.

36 Joann Vanek, Canadian Broadcasting Corporation radio interview, 13 November 1974, CBC archives online.

37 Michael Bittman, James Mahmud Rice and Judy Wajcman, 'Appliances and Their Impact: the ownership of domestic technology and time spent on household work', Social Policy Research Centre, UNSW, discussion paper No. 129, October 2003.

38 Alex Martin, littlebrowndress.com.

39 'Japanese men shirk housework', BBC News Online, 13 March 2002.

40 Lyn Craig, op. cit.

41 Ruth Cowan, op. cit.

42 Bettina Arndt, 'Stop putting down the dads', *Herald Sun,* 23 July 2007, p18.

43 Bettina Arndt, 'Avoid more marital mess with a clean sweep of housework', *The Canberra Times,* 14 September 2007, p1.

44 Stephen Lunn, 'Dads give kids a minute a weekday', The Australian, 20 October 2008, p3.

45 Janeen Baxter and Mark Western, 'Satisfaction with Housework: Examining the Paradox', ANU, November 1996; Ken Dempsey, 'Men and Women's Power Relationships and the Persisting Inequitable Division of Housework', La Trobe University, November 1998.

46 Viv Groskop, 'Escape from the Past', *The Guardian,* 18 April 2009.

47 ABS survey, March 2008, quoted in Jessica Irvine, 'Mums still home, despite the hype', *The Sydney Morning Herald,* 26 March 2008, p3.

48 Matthew Perkins, 'A man's place is in the home', ABC Radio 720 Perth, 2 April 2008.

49 'Working mums prefer to stay home with kids', *The Daily Telegraph*, 26 August 2008.

50 Quentin Bryce, opening address, Queensland Alliance Mental Health Forum, Salvation Army Conference Centre, Stafford, 26 November 2004.

51 John Carvel, 'Two into one won't go: Cambridge survey shows new doubts over working mothers', *The Guardian*, 6 August 2008.

52 Antonia Kidman, op. cit.

53 David Smiedt, 'How to get children to do household chores', *Sunday Life* magazine, *The Sun Herald*, 28 September 2008.

54 Matthew Perkins, op. cit.

55 Hawkins Pressure Cookery instruction book, Brahm Vasudeva for Hawkins Cookers Ltd, Bombay, 1987.

56 *Oxford English Dictionary*, second edition, volume XII, 1989.

57 *Oxford Dictionary of National Biography*, Vol 42, Oxford University Press, 2004.

58 *Oxford English Dictionary*, op. cit.

59 Margaret Fulton, *I Sang for My Supper: Memoirs of a Food Writer*, Lansdowne Publishing, 1999.

60 Brian Hill, *Wirraway to Hornet: A History of the Commonwealth Aircraft Corporation*, Southern Cross Publishing, 1998.

61 Margaret Fulton, op. cit.

62 John Lack, 'Storey, Sir John Stanley (1896–1955)', in D. Langmore (ed), *Australian Dictionary of Biography*, Volume 16, Melbourne University Press, 2002, pp 319–323.